ONDORI
DANISH CROS

M000248763

CONTENTS

★Published by Ondorisha Publishers Ltd.
 32 Nishigoken-cho, Shinjuku-ku, Tokyo 162, Japan.
★Sole Overseas Distributor: Japan Publications Trading Co., Ltd.
 P.O.Box 5030 Tokyo International, Tokyo, Japan.
★Distributed in the United States by Kodansha International/USA Ltd.
 through Harper & Row, Publishers, Inc., 10 East 53rd Street, New York, New York 10022.
 Australia by Bookwise International, 1 Jeanes Street, Beverley, South Australia 5009, Australia.

10 9 8 7 6 5 4 3

★ISBN 0-87040-627-2
 Printed in Japan

FLORAL MOTIFS

Rose Tablecloth
Instructions on page 33.

1

Daisy Tablecloth and Napkin Set
Instructions on page 36.

Violet Placemat and Napkin Set
Instructions on page 45.

Garland Tablecloth
Instructions on page 38.

4

Wreath Table Center
Instructions on page 40.

Anemone Table Center
Instructions on page 43.

Wall Hanging
Instructions on page 42.

8

Piano Cover
Instructions on page 46.

Leaf Pillow
Instructions on page 48.

Flower Pillow
Instructions on page 50.

11

MOTIFS FROM NATURE

Leaf Wall Hanging
Instructions on page 52.

Bedspread
Instructions on page 55.

House Panel
Instructions on page 58.

Framed Flowers
Instructions on page 60.

Sweet Memories

Floral Album Cover
Instructions on page 62.

Black Velvet Bag
Instructions on page 67.

Primrose Album Cover
Instructions on page 64.

Leaf Pochette
Instructions on page 66.

Table Center and Napkin Set
Instructions on page 70.

My Happy Time

Coasters
Instructions on page 69.

Pansy Doily
Instructions on page 74.

Blue Doily
Instructions on page 73.

21

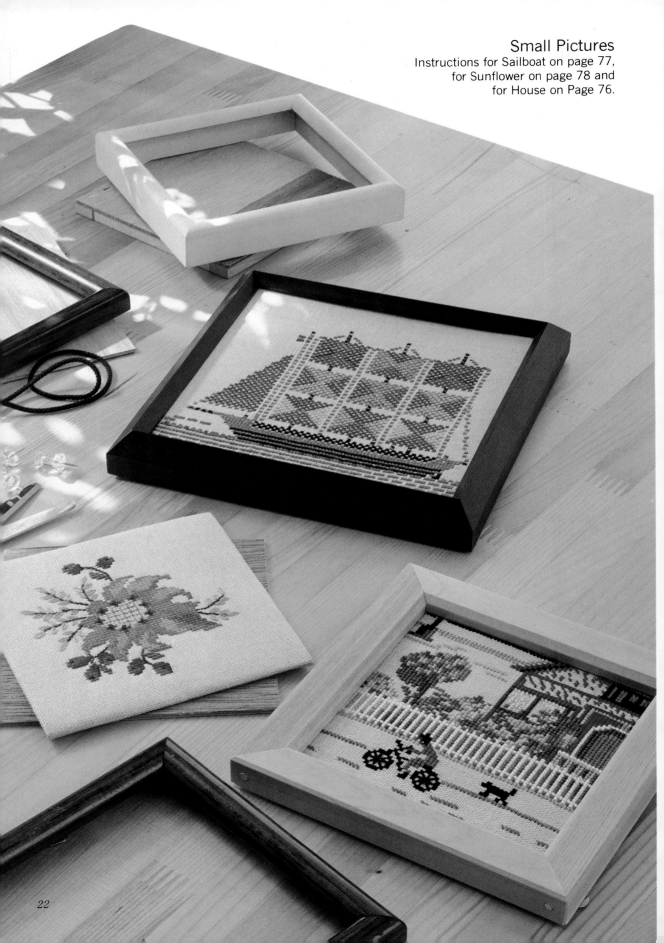

Small Pictures
Instructions for Sailboat on page 77,
for Sunflower on page 78 and
for House on Page 76.

Petunia Doily
Instructions on page 80.

Framed Petunia
Instructions on page 79.

Bluebird
and Flower Runner
Instructions on page 82.

Bluebird and Flower Table Center
Instructions on page 86.

Bird and Flower Pillows
Instructions on page 88.

Pochette
Instructions on page 90.

USEFUL SMALL ITEMS

a

b

c

g

WITH 2 STRANDS.

DMC
ART 117

oehlenschl

28

Pincushions

Instructions for (a) and (b) on page 93, for (c) and (d) on page 94, and for (e) and (f) on page 91.

Scissors Cases

Instructions for (g) on page 98 and for (h) on page 96.

Instructions for (a) and (b) on page 54, and for (c), (d) and (e) on page 99.

Cosmetic Cases
Instructions for (f) and (g) on page 100 and for (h), (i) and (j) on page 101.

h   i

j

g

31

Shoulder Bag (a)
Instructions on page 106.

a

BERRIES

Tote Bag (b)
Instructions on page 104.

b

INSTRUCTIONS

* Bold faced numbers indicate dimension in centimeter.
* Light faced numbers indicate numbers of threads of the fabric.

Rose Tablecloth *shown on page 1.*

Materials:
Fabric: White Indian cloth (52 mesh to 10cm), 91cm square.
Thread: D.M.C. 6-strand embroidery floss, No. 25. See the arrow for colors and amount.
Finished Size: 84cm square.

Directions: Match centers of fabric and design, and cross-stitch as indicated. Draw 4 threads from fabric crosswise and lengthwise, turn edges back twice and hem with white sewing thread, mitering corners.

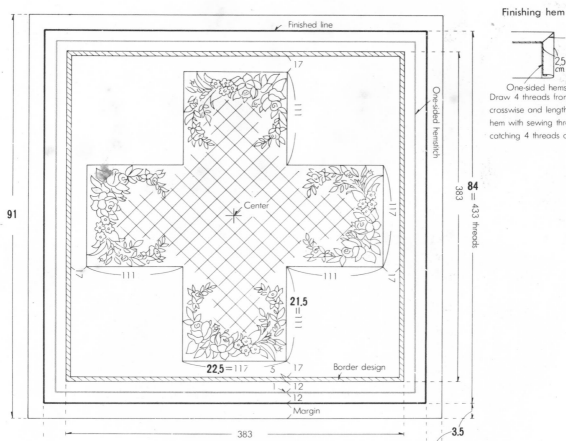

Finishing hem

One-sided hemstitch
Draw 4 threads from fabric crosswise and lengthwise, hem with sewing thread, catching 4 threads at a time.

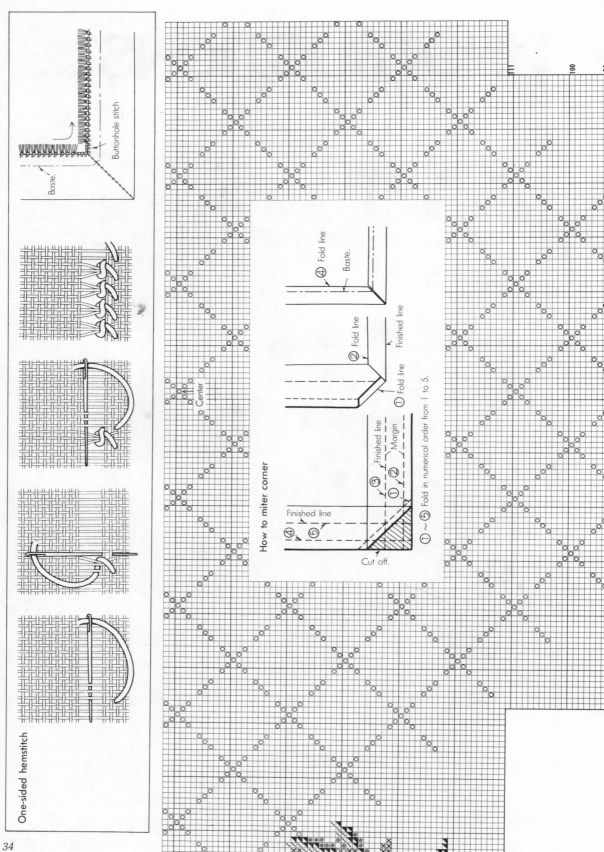

One-sided hemstitch

Buttonhole stitch

Baste.

How to miter corner

④ Fold line

Baste.

② Fold line

Finished line

① Fold line

Center

③ Finished line

② Margin

①

Finished line

④ ⑤

Cut off.

① ~ ⑤ Fold in numerical order from 1 to 5.

100

94

34

Border design

Center

One square of design equals one square mesh of fabric.

↑ **Color Key**

Use 4 strands of floss.
Required amount is shown in
brackets.

Green
S = 733 [4 skeins]
|| = 3012 [4 skeins]
⊠ = 3011 [4 skeins]
⁄ = 989 [4 skeins]
✗ = 988 [4 skeins]
◣ = 935 [4 skeins]

Purple
| = 211 [2 skeins]
▨ = 210 [2 skeins]
⊠ = 208 [2 skeins]

Rose
• = 818 [4 skeins]
L = 3689 [4 skeins]
□ = 3688 [4 skeins]
◕ = 3687 [4 skeins]
■ = 3685 [4 skeins]
T = 899 [4 skeins]
◣ = 309 [4 skeins]
● = 326 [4 skeins]

Hazelnut
brown ○ = 869 [7 skeins]

Saffron ⊠ = 726 [1 skein]

Daisy Tablecloth and Napkin Set *shown on pages 2 & 3.*

Materials:

Fabric: Beige Java canvas (41 mesh to 10cm), 90cm by 354cm for tablecloth and 46cm square for napkin.

Thread: D.M.C. 6-strand embroidery floss, No. 25. See the arrow for colors and amount.

Finished Size: Tablecloth, 170cm by 133.5cm. Napkin, 40cm square.

Directions:

For Tablecloth: Cut fabric and sew pieces together to get one piece of the designated size, matching grain. Embroider as indicated, matching centers of fabric and design. Turn edges back twice and hem, mitering corners.

For Napkin: Embroider as indicated. Turn edges back twice and hem, mitering corners.

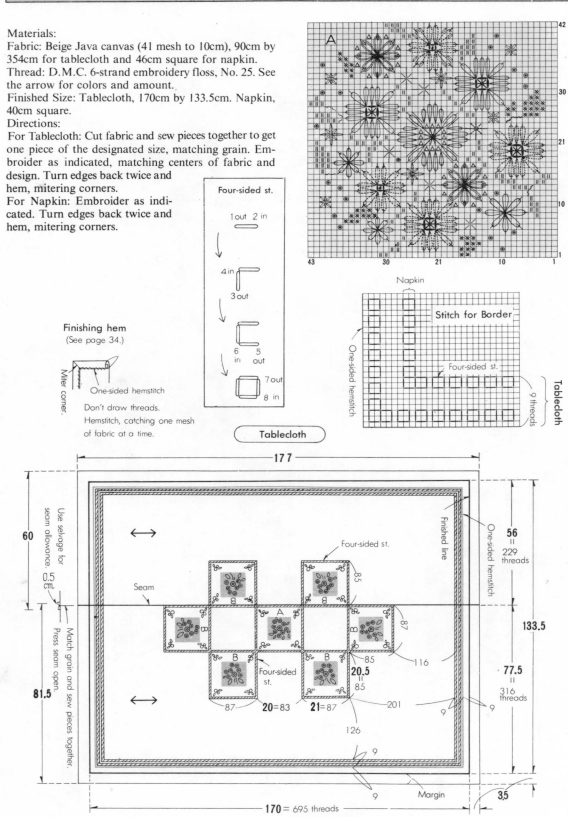

Finishing hem
(See page 34.)

Miter corner.

One-sided hemstitch

Don't draw threads.
Hemstitch, catching one mesh of fabric at a time.

Four-sided st.

1 out   2 in

4 in
3 out

6   5
in   out

7 out
8 in

Tablecloth

Napkin

Stitch for Border

One-sided hemstitch

Four-sided st.

9 threads

Tablecloth

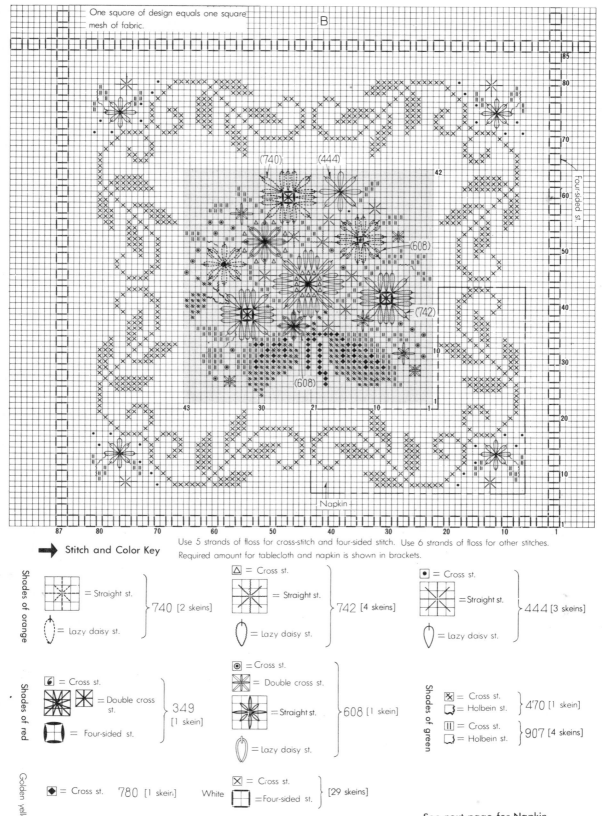

One square of design equals one square mesh of fabric.

B

85
80
70
42
60
(740)   (444)
(608)
50
(742)
40
10
30
1
(608)
43   30   21   10   1
20
Napkin
10
1
87 80   70   60   50   40   30   20   10   1

Four-sided st.

➡ **Stitch and Color Key**

Use 5 strands of floss for cross-stitch and four-sided stitch. Use 6 strands of floss for other stitches.
Required amount for tablecloth and napkin is shown in brackets.

Shades of orange
⊛ = Straight st.
◞ = Lazy daisy st.
} 740 [2 skeins]

△ = Cross st.
✳ = Straight st.
◞ = Lazy daisy st.
} 742 [4 skeins]

⊡ = Cross st.
⊛ = Straight st.
◞ = Lazy daisy st.
} 444 [3 skeins]

Shades of red
◢ = Cross st.
✸ ✷ = Double cross st.
⊟ = Four-sided st.
} 349 [1 skein]

◉ = Cross st.
✳ = Double cross st.
✳ = Straight st.
◞ = Lazy daisy st.
} 608 [1 skein]

Shades of green
☒ = Cross st.
▱ = Holbein st.
} 470 [1 skein]
‖ = Cross st.
▭ = Holbein st.
} 907 [4 skeins]

Golden yellow
◆ = Cross st.   780 [1 skein]

White
☒ = Cross st.
⊞ = Four-sided st.
} [29 skeins]

See next page for Napkin.

37

Napkin

46

40

Front side st.

Finished line

40

8

10

2

Margin

3

Finishing hem

Slip-stitch.

Miter corner (see page 34).

2 cm

Finishing hem

Slip-stitch.

3 cm

Miter corner (see page 34)

Garland Tablecloth *shown on page 5.*

Materials:
Fabric: Beige Java canvas (41 mesh to 10cm), 90cm by 352cm.
Thread: D.M.C. 6-strand embroidery floss, No. 25. See the arrow for colors and amount.

Finished Size: 166 cm by 130cm.
Directions: Cut fabric and sew pieces together to get one piece of the designated size. Match centers of fabric and design, and cross-stitch as indicated. Turn edges back twice and hem, mitering corners.

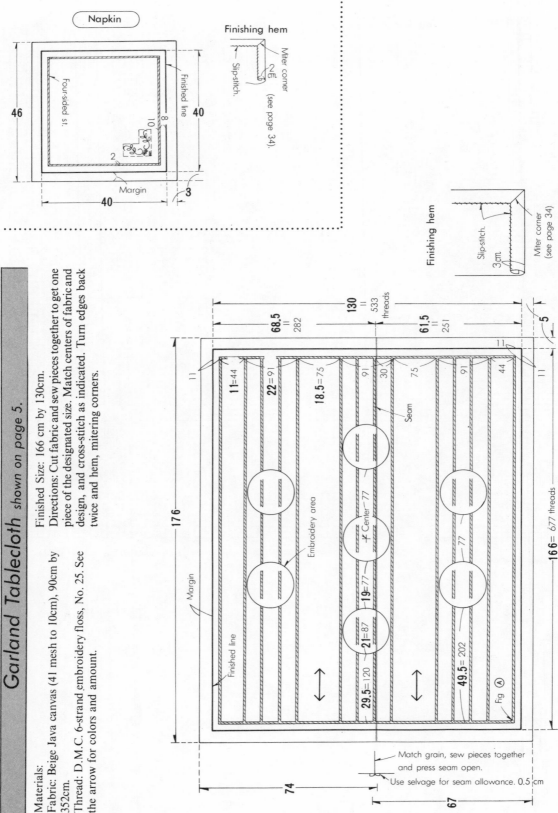

130 = 533 threads

68.5 = 282

61.5 = 251

5

11

11=44

22

16

18.5=75

91

30

75

91

44

11

176

Margin

Finished line

Embroidery area

Seam

Center 77

29.5=120

21=87

19=77

77

49.5=202

Fig Ⓐ

166 = 677 threads

Match grain, sew pieces together and press seam open.
Use selvage for seam allowance. 0.5 cm

74

67

38

Color Key Use 6 strands of floss.

Required amount is shown in brackets.

Yellow

- ⁄ = 307 [7 skeins]
- ◎ = 741 [4 skeins]
- + = 743 [3 skeins]

Shades of red

- ● = 817 [3 skeins]
- ✕ = 350 [1.5 skeins]

Green

- ◢ = 988
- = 988 Holbein st. } [6 skeins]
- ◢ = 3011
- = 3011 Holbein st. } [5 skeins]
- I = 3348 [4 skeins]
- = = 733 [3.5 skeins]

Shades of brown

- ◆ = 780
- = 780 Holbein st. } [17 skeins]
- ※ = 833
- = 833 Holbein st. } [6.5 skeins]

Center
Seam
One square of design equals one square mesh of fabric.
91
80
60
40
20
1
87

Fig. Ⓐ

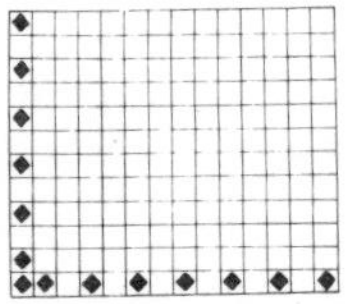

Materials:

Fabric: Beige congress canvas (70 mesh to 10cm), 51cm by 126cm.

Thread: D.M.C. retors a broder. See the arrow for colors and amount.

Finished Size: 116cm by 41cm.

Directions: Match centers of fabric and design, and embroider as indicated. Turn edges back twice, machine-stitch folded edges and slip-stitch.

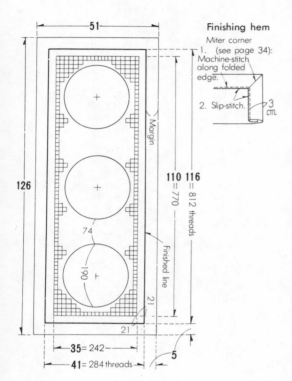

Finishing hem

Miter corner
1. (see page 34): Machine-stitch along folded edge.

2. Slip-stitch.   3 cm

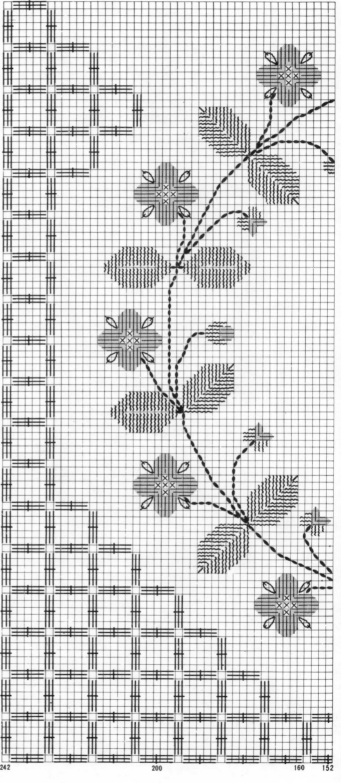

Stitch and Color Key   Use one strand of floss.

Required amount is shown in brackets.

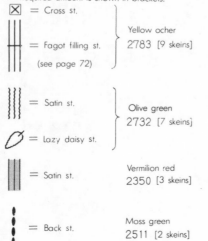

☒	= Cross st.	
	= Fagot filling st.	Yellow ocher
	(see page 72)	2783 [9 skeins]

| | = Satin st. | Olive green |
| ⬭ | = Lazy daisy st. | 2732 [7 skeins] |

| | = Satin st. | Vermilion red 2350 [3 skeins] |

| ⦙ | = Back st. | Moss green 2511 [2 skeins] |

242   200   160 152

40

Center

One square of design equals
two square mesh of fabric.

230

200

160

120

80

40

1

150

120

80

40

1

Materials:

Fabric: Beige Java canvas (35 mesh to 10cm), 68cm by 31cm.

Thread: D.M.C. 6-strand embroidery floss, No. 25. See the arrow for colors and amount.

Notions: Iron-on interfacing, 63cm by 14cm. Bias tape, 1.2cm wide and 32cm long. Bellpull attachments, one pair.

Finished Size: 63cm by 14 cm (excluding bellpull attachments).

Directions: Match centers of fabric and design, and cross-stitch. Press iron-on interfacing on wrong side of embroidered piece. Make up for wall hanging, following diagrams below.

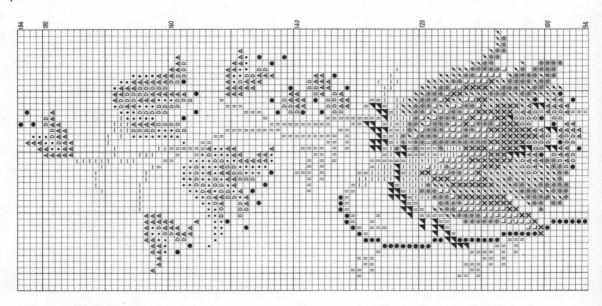

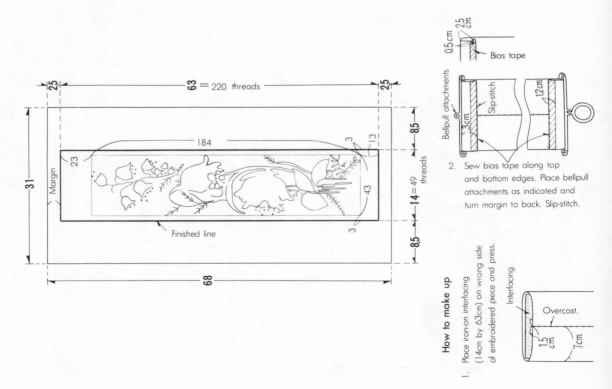

How to make up

1. Place iron-on interfacing (14cm by 63cm) on wrong side of embroidered piece and press.

2. Sew bias tape along top and bottom edges. Place bellpull attachments as indicated and turn margin to back. Slip-stitch.

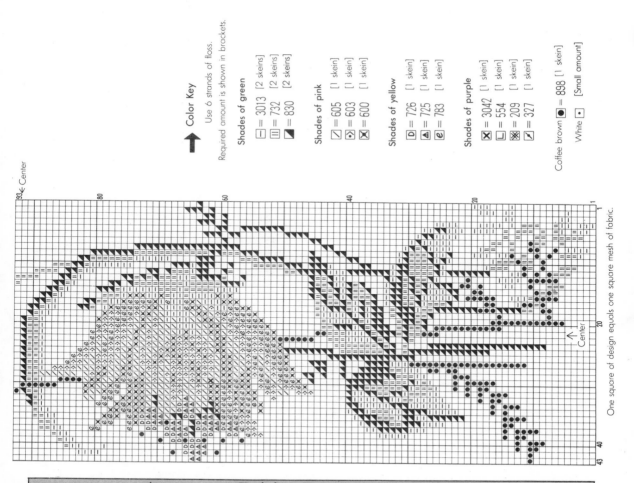

Anemone Table Center *shown on page 7.*

Materials:
Fabric: White Java canvas (41 mesh to 10cm), 89.5cm by 38.5cm.
Thread: D.M.C. 6-strand embroidery floss, No. 25. See the arrow for colors and amount.

Finished Size: 82.5cm by 31.5cm.
Directions: Match centers of fabric and design, and cross-stitch. Turn edges back twice and slip-stitch, mitering corners.

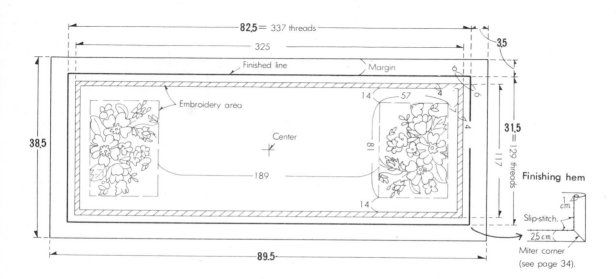

Color Key Use 5 strands of floss.   Required amount is shown in brackets.

Green

s	= 3348	[1 skein]
✕	= 906	[1 skein]
◐	= 3346	[4 skeins]
▲	= 986	[1 skein]

Pink

I	= 963	[2 skeins]
◉	= 894	[2 skeins]
◎	= 893	[1 skein]
●	= 891	[1 skein]

Blue

•	= 800	[1 skein]
e	= 798	[1 skein]
+	= 797	[2 skeins]
■	= 796	[1 skein]

Saffron □ = 725 [0.5 skein]
Golden yellow ▲ = 783 [0.5 skein]

One square of design equals one square mesh of fabric.

57 threads

81 threads

Center

44

Materials (for 2 pieces each):
Fabric: Beige Java canvas (35 mesh to 10cm), 77cm by 50cm for 2 placemats; 78cm by 39cm for 2 napkins.
Thread: D.M.C. 6-strand embroidery floss, No. 25. See the arrow for colors and amount.
Finished Size: Placemat, 47cm by 35.5cm. Napkin, 36cm square.

Directions:
For Placemat: Match centers of fabric and design, and cross-stitch. Turn edges back twice and slip-stitch.
For Napkin: Cross-stitch as indicated. Turn edges back twice and slip-stitch.

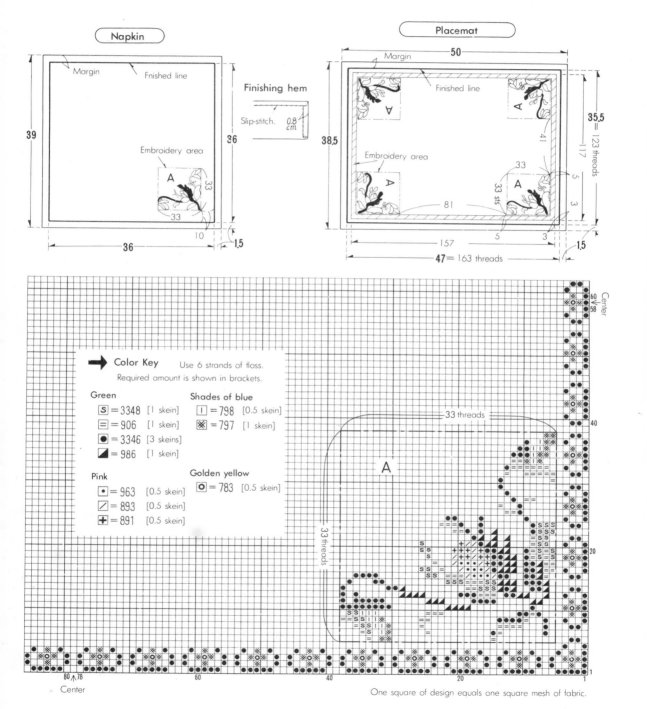

Color Key Use 6 strands of floss.
Required amount is shown in brackets.

Green
S = 3348 [1 skein]
= 906 [1 skein]
● = 3346 [3 skeins]
◢ = 986 [1 skein]

Pink
• = 963 [0.5 skein]
∕ = 893 [0.5 skein]
+ = 891 [0.5 skein]

Shades of blue
I = 798 [0.5 skein]
✕ = 797 [1 skein]

Golden yellow
O = 783 [0.5 skein]

One square of design equals one square mesh of fabric.

Piano Cover *shown on page 9.*

Materials:
Fabric: Beige Java canvas (41 mesh to 10cm), 91cm by 221cm.
Thread: D.M.C. 6-strand embroidery floss, No. 25. See the arrow for colors and amount.

Finished Size: 213.5cm by 84cm.
Directions: Cross-stitch as indicated. Turn edges back twice and slip-stitch, mitering corners.

➡ **Color Key**   I Use 5 strands of floss. (Use 2 strands of floss for Holbein St.)   Required amount is shown in brackets.

Green
- ■ = 895 [1 skein]
- II = 905
- ⊐ = 905 Holbein st. } [5 skeins]
- ✖ = 701 [2 skeins]
- ⌒ = 702 [2 skeins]
- ⊙ = 3346 [3 skeins]
- ⊟ = 907 [3 skeins]

Blue
- ◆ = 798 [1 skein]
- ✖ = 793 [1 skein]
- ✐ = 794 [1 skein]
- △ = 800 [1 skein]

Shades of pink
- ◎ = 602
- ☐ = 602 Holbein st. } [2 skeins]
- · = 776 [1 skein]

Shades of yellow
- Z = 725 [1 skein]
- ⊘ = 726 [2 skeins]

Golden yellow 6 = 782 [1 skein]

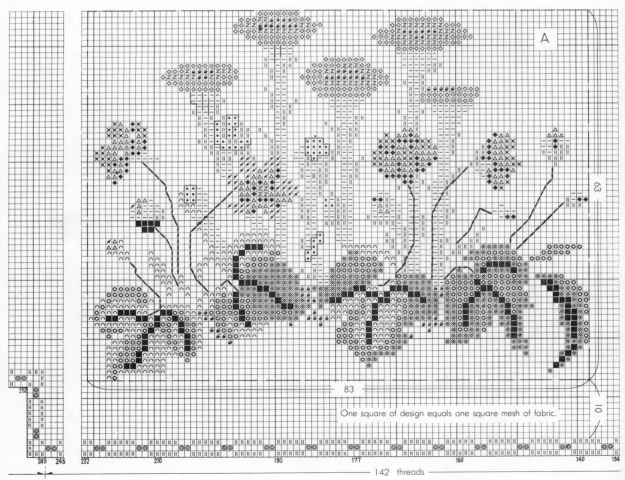

83

One square of design equals one square mesh of fabric.

142 threads

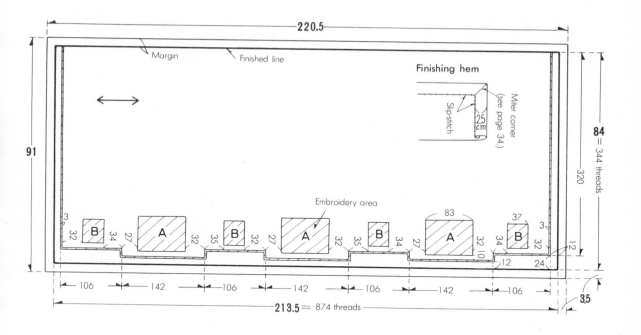

220.5

Margin   Finished line

Finishing hem

Slipstitch   Miter corner (see page 34)   2.5 cm

84 = 344 threads

320

91

Embroidery area

3
32 B 34 27 A 32 35 B 32 27 A 32 35 B 34 27 A 32 34 B 32 3
83   37
32 10
12 24
12

3.5

|← 106 →|← 142 →|← 106 →|← 142 →|← 106 →|← 142 →|← 106 →|

213.5 = 874 threads

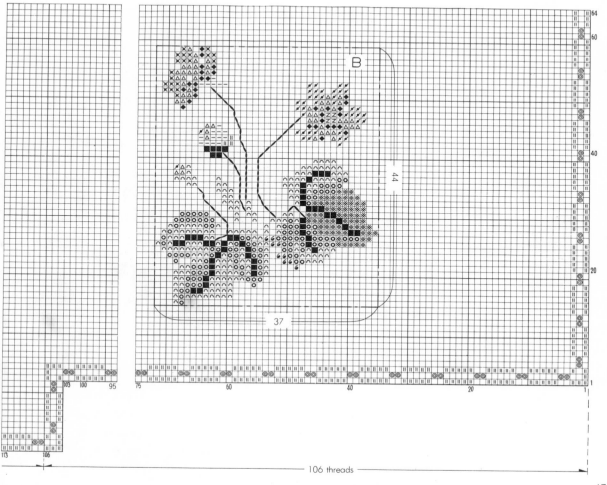

B

44

37

113 106
103 100 95
75   60   40   20   1

106 threads

64
60
40
20
1

Leaf Pillow
shown on page 10.

Materials:

Fabric: Beige Indian cloth (52 mesh to 10cm), 83cm by 46cm.

Thread: D.M.C. 6-strand embroidery floss, No. 25. See the arrow for colors and amount.

Notions: Inner pillow, 40.5cm by 43cm, stuffed with 400g of kapok. Zipper, 39cm long. Brown cotton cord, 1cm in diameter and 200cm long.

Finished Size: 39.5cm by 42cm.

Directions: Match centers of fabric and design, and cross-stitch. Sew ends (1.5cm each) of back pieces together and sew on zipper. Sew front and back pieces together with right sides facing. Turn inside out and sew on cord. Insert inner pillow.

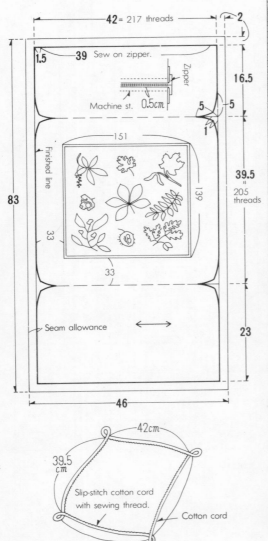

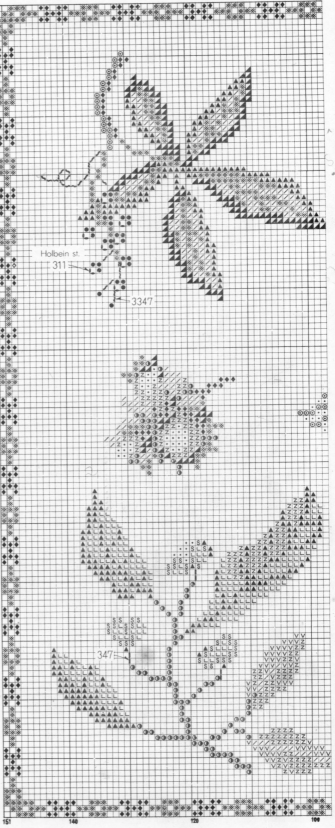

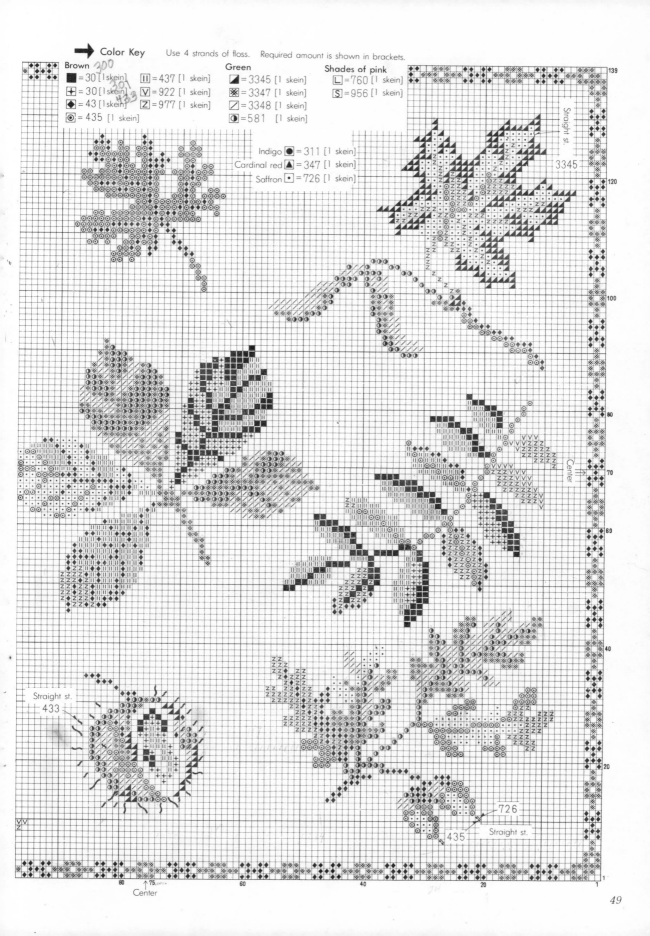

Color Key   Use 4 strands of floss.   Required amount is shown in brackets.

Brown
■ = 301 [1 skein]
⊞ = 30 [1 skein]
◆ = 43 [1 skein]
◉ = 435 [1 skein]

Ⅱ = 437 [1 skein]
Ⅴ = 922 [1 skein]
Ⅻ = 977 [1 skein]

Green
◩ = 3345 [1 skein]
⊠ = 3347 [1 skein]
⧄ = 3348 [1 skein]
◑ = 581 [1 skein]

Shades of pink
Ⅼ = 760 [1 skein]
Ⅾ = 956 [1 skein]

Indigo ● = 311 [1 skein]
Cardinal red ▲ = 347 [1 skein]
Saffron • = 726 [1 skein]

Straight st.
3345

Straight st.
433

Center

726
435
Straight st.

Center

Flower Pillow *shown on page 11.*

Materials (for one):

Fabric: Beige Java canvas (35 mesh to 10cm), 38cm by 32cm. Dark green (or dark brown) velveteen, 90 cm by 130cm.

Thread: D.M.C. 6-strand embroidery floss, No. 25. See the arrow for colors and amount.

Notions: Braid, 115cm long. Inner pillow, 52cm by 42cm, stuffed with 550g of kapok. Small amount of bulky yarn.

Finished Size: 58 cm by 48cm (including ruffle).

Directions: Match centers of Java canvas and design, and cross-stitch. Cut velveteen as indicated. Turn in seam allowance of Java canvas, place it onto front of velveteen and machine-stitch. Sew on braid along embroidered piece. Sew zipper onto back pieces. Sew front and back pieces together with right sides facing. Turn inside out. Sew pieces for ruffle together. Sew on ruffle in slip stitch. Insert inner pillow.

Java canvas for embroidery

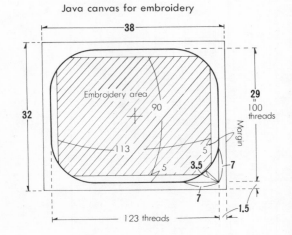

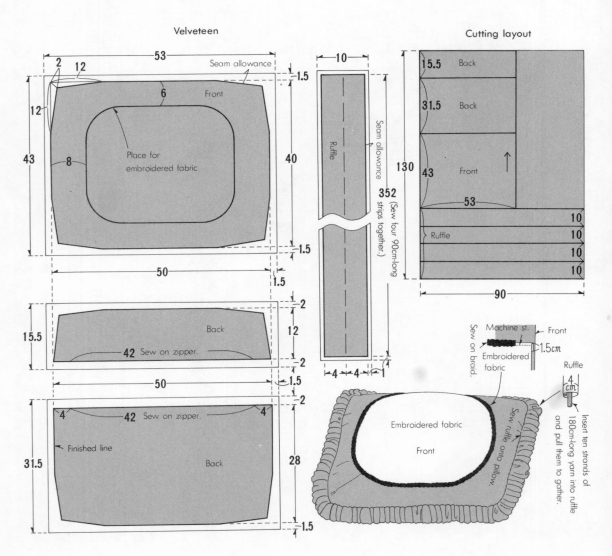

Velveteen

Cutting layout

50

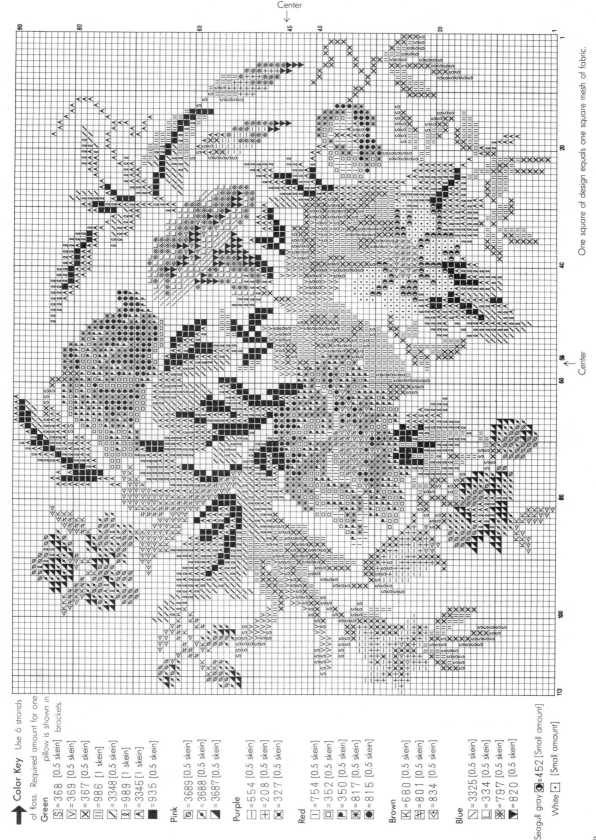

One square of design equals one square mesh of fabric.

Center

Center

Color Key Use 6 strands of floss. Required amount for one pillow is shown in brackets.

Green
S = 368 [0.5 skein]
V = 369 [0.5 skein]
X = 367 [0.5 skein]
||| = 986 [1 skein]
/ = 3348 [0.5 skein]
Q = 989 [1 skein]
A = 3345 [1 skein]
■ = 935 [0.5 skein]

Pink
Ø = 3689 [0.5 skein]
◪ = 3688 [0.5 skein]
◥ = 3687 [0.5 skein]

Purple
| = 554 [0.5 skein]
+ = 208 [0.5 skein]
X = 327 [0.5 skein]

Red
I = 754 [0.5 skein]
□ = 352 [0.5 skein]
◨ = 350 [0.5 skein]
✳ = 817 [0.5 skein]
● = 815 [0.5 skein]

Brown
K = 680 [0.5 skein]
⊞ = 801 [0.5 skein]
◁ = 834 [0.5 skein]

Blue
▽ = 3325 [0.5 skein]
L = 334 [0.5 skein]
✕ = 797 [0.5 skein]
▼ = 820 [0.5 skein]

Seagull gray ◉ = 452 [Small amount]

White · = [Small amount]

Leaf Wall Hanging *shown on page 12.*

Materials:

Fabric: Beige congress canvas (70 mesh to 10cm), 90cm by 75cm.

Thread: D.M.C. 6-strand embroidery floss, No. 25. See the arrow for colors and amount.

Notions: Two dowels, 1.2cm in diameter and 45cm long each. Cord, 0.4cm in diameter and 80cm long.

Finished Size: 40cm wide and 61cm long.

Directions: Match centers of fabric and design, and cross-stitch. With right sides facing, fold in half lengthwise and sew side seam. Bring seam to center back and press seam open. Turn inside out. Turn top and bottom edges to back and slip-stitch. Insert dowels into casings. Tie cord for hanging.

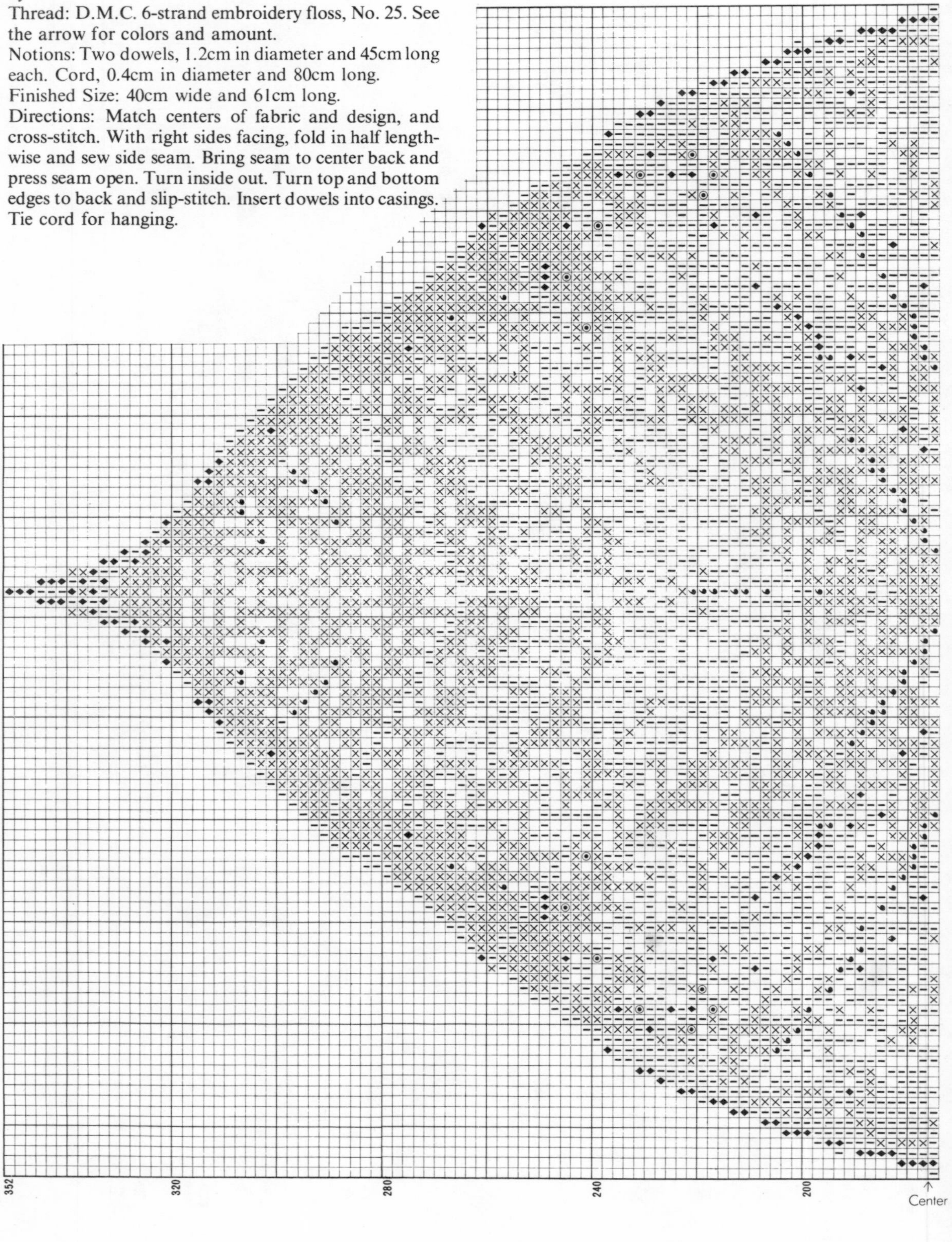

352 320 280 240 200

↑
Center

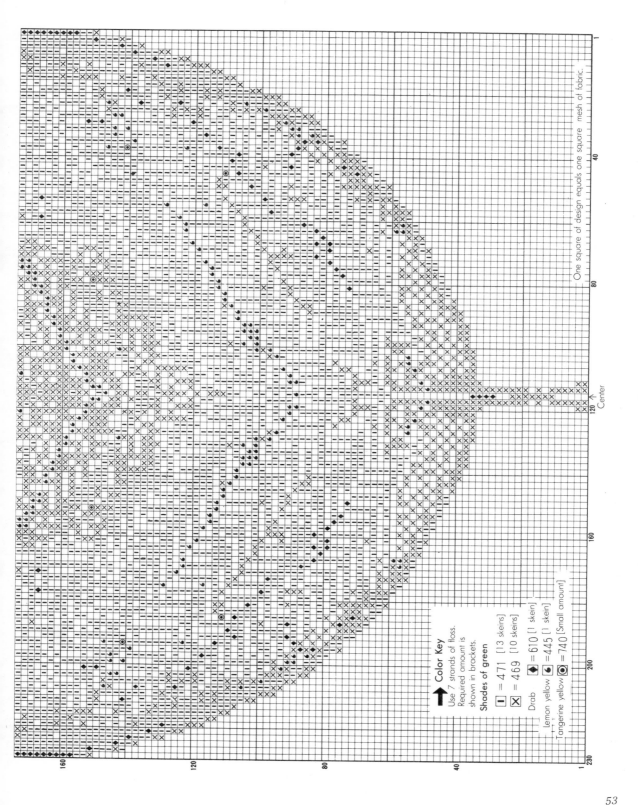

Color Key

Use 7 strands of floss.
Required amount is
shown in brackets.

Shades of green

I	= 471	[13 skeins]
X	= 469	[10 skeins]

Drab ◆	= 610	[1 skein]
Lemon yellow ●	= 445	[1 skein]
Tangerine yellow ◉	= 740	[Small amount]

One square of design equals one square mesh of fabric.

Center

53

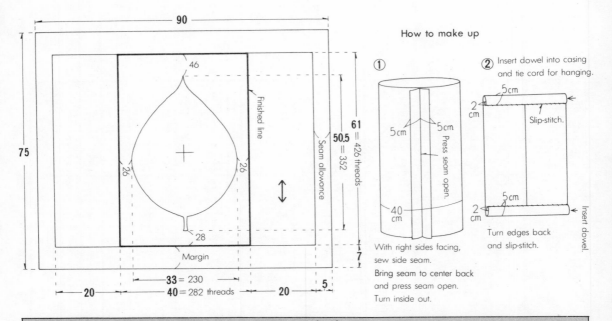

How to make up

① With right sides facing, sew side seam.
Bring seam to center back and press seam open.
Turn inside out.

② Insert dowel into casing and tie cord for hanging.
Turn edges back and slip-stitch.

Tissue Cases (a) and (b) *shown on page 30.*

Materials (for one):
Fabric: Blue (pink) Indian cloth (52 mesh to 10cm), 14.5cm by 23cm. Cotton broadcloth for lining, 14.5cm by 18cm.
Thread: D.M.C. 6-strand embroidery floss, No. 25. See the arrow for colors and amount.

Finished Size: 12.5cm by 9 cm.
Directions: Match centers of fabric and design, and cross-stitch. Make up for Tissue Case following diagrams below.

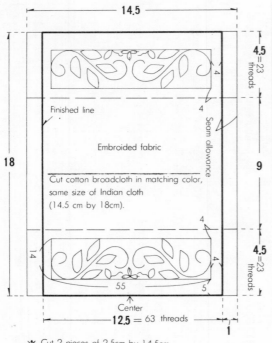

※ Cut 2 pieces of 2.5cm by 14.5cm from Indian cloth.

How to make up

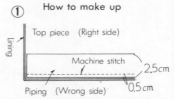

① With wrong sides of Indian cloth and cotton broadcloth together, place strip on top and stitch.

② Turn strip to back, turn in seam allowance and stitch in the ditch from front.

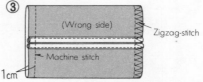

③ Fold lined piece as shown with right sides facing and stitch each side. Zigzag-stitch along edges. Turn to right side.

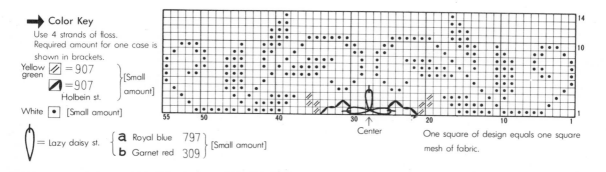

➡ **Color Key**

Use 4 strands of floss.
Required amount for one case is
shown in brackets.

Yellow green ⊘ = 907 } [Small amount]
◥ = 907
Holbein st.

White [•] [Small amount]

◊ = Lazy daisy st. { **a** Royal blue 797 } [Small amount]
{ **b** Garnet red 309 }

One square of design equals one square
mesh of fabric.

Bedspread *shown on page 13.*

Materials:
Fabric: Beige Java canvas (30 mesh to 10cm), 67cm by
307cm. Reversible quilted fabric, 100cm by 615cm.
Thread: D.M.C. 6-strand embroidery floss, No. 25. See
the arrow for colors and amount.
Notions: Braid, 16.1m long. Bias tape, 1.8cm wide and
10m long.

Finished Size: 307cm by 196cm.
Directions: Match centers of fabric and design, and
cross-stitch. Join two pieces of quilted fabric and press
seam open. Place embroidered piece on quilted fabric
and slip-stitch. Bind edges with bias tape. Sew on braid
as shown in diagram.

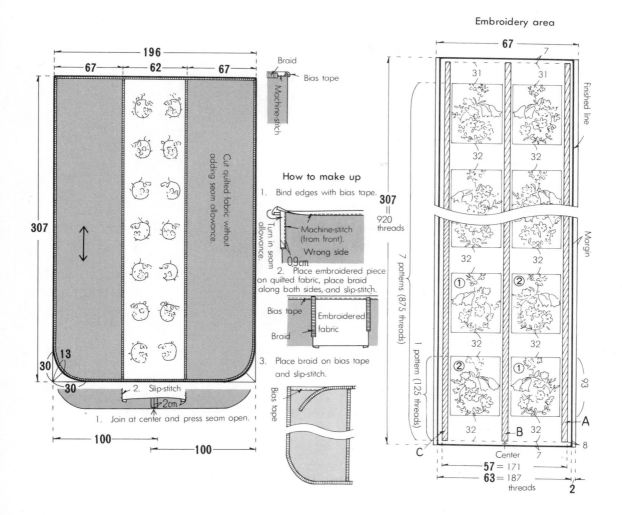

How to make up

1. Bind edges with bias tape.
2. Place embroidered piece on quilted fabric, place braid along both sides, and slip-stitch.
3. Place braid on bias tape and slip-stitch.

Embroidery area

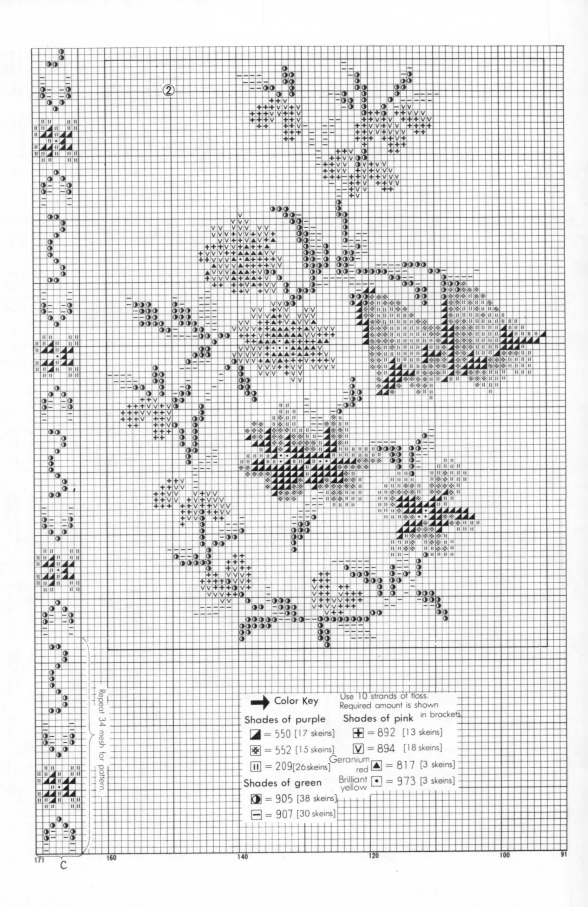

②

Repeat 34 mesh for pattern.

➡ Color Key

Use 10 strands of floss.
Required amount is shown
in brackets

Shades of purple

◪ = 550 [17 skeins]

✴ = 552 [15 skeins]

‖ = 209 [26 skeins]

Shades of green

◑ = 905 [38 skeins]

⊟ = 907 [30 skeins]

Shades of pink

➕ = 892 [13 skeins]

▼ = 894 [18 skeins]

Geranium red ▲ = 817 [3 skeins]

Brilliant yellow • = 973 [3 skeins]

171   160   140   120   100   91

C

One square of design equals one square mesh of fabric.

Repeat 34 meshes for pattern.

Repeat 34 meshes for pattern.

57

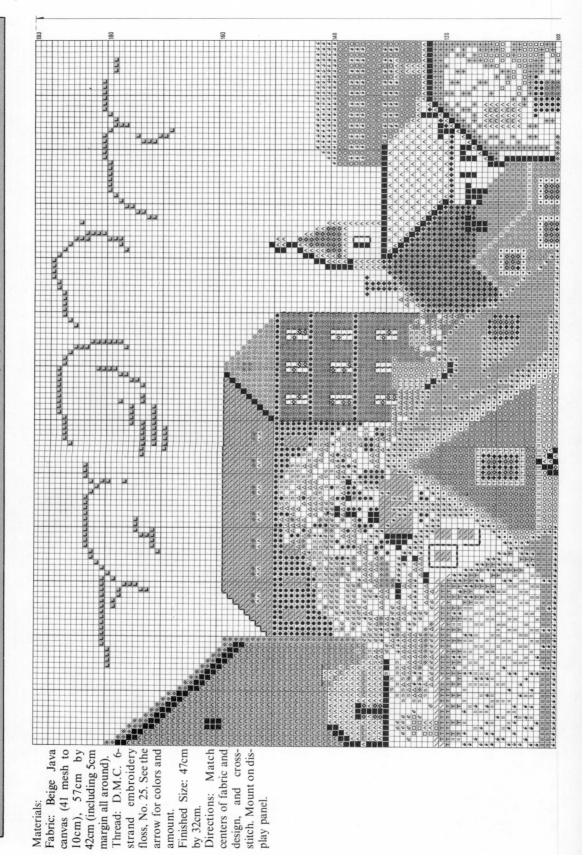

Materials:
Fabric: Beige Java canvas (41 mesh to 10cm), 57cm by 42cm (including 5cm margin all around).
Thread: D.M.C. 6-strand embroidery floss, No. 25. See the arrow for colors and amount.
Finished Size: 47cm by 32cm.
Directions: Match centers of fabric and design, and cross-stitch. Mount on display panel.

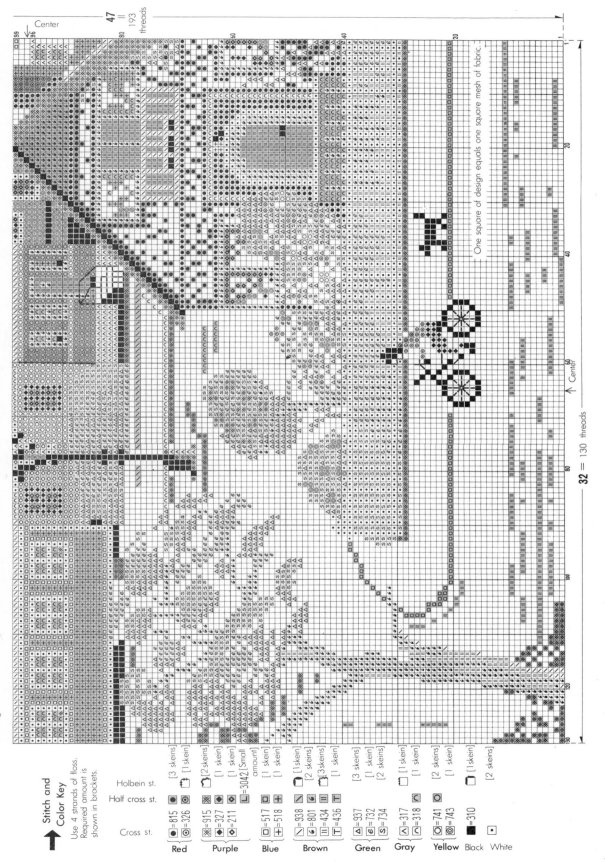

Center
47 = 193 threads

One square of design equals one square mesh of fabric.

Center
32 = 130 threads

Stitch and Color Key

Use 4 strands of floss.
Required amount is shown in brackets.

Holbein st.	[3 skeins]	[1 skein]	
Half cross st.			
Cross st.			

Red: ● =815 [2 skeins] ◎ =326 [1 skein]
Purple: ▨ =915 [1 skein] ◆ =327 ◇ =211 [1 skein]
3042 [Small amount]
Blue: ☐ =517 [1 skein] ✚ =518 [1 skein]
Brown: ◨ =938 [2 skeins] ◩ =801 [3 skeins] T =434 T =436 [1 skein]
Green: ◮ =937 [3 skeins] ◷ =732 [1 skein] ◿ =734 [2 skeins]
Gray: ◁ =317 [1 skein] C =318 [1 skein]
Yellow: ◎ =741 [2 skeins] ◉ =743 [1 skein]
Black: ■ =310 [2 skeins]
White: ·

59

Framed Flowers *shown on page 15.*

Materials:
Fabric: Beige Indian cloth (52 mesh to 10cm), 45cm by 36cm.

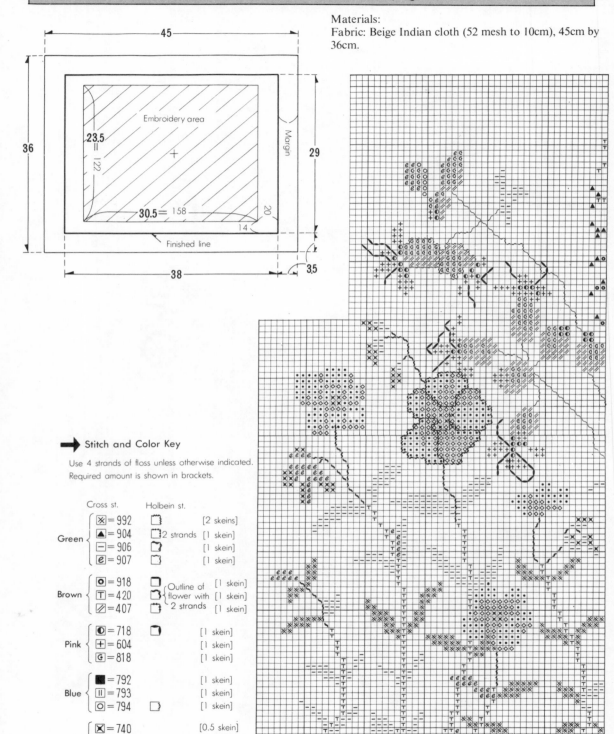

Stitch and Color Key

Use 4 strands of floss unless otherwise indicated.
Required amount is shown in brackets.

	Cross st.	Holbein st.	
Green	⊠ = 992	☐	[2 skeins]
	▲ = 904	☐ 2 strands	[1 skein]
	— = 906	☐	[1 skein]
	ℓ = 907	☐	[1 skein]
Brown	◐ = 918	☐ Outline of	[1 skein]
	T = 420	☐ flower with	[1 skein]
	▨ = 407	☐ 2 strands	[1 skein]
Pink	◑ = 718	☐	[1 skein]
	+ = 604		[1 skein]
	G = 818		[1 skein]
Blue	■ = 792		[1 skein]
	‖ = 793		[1 skein]
	◎ = 794	☐	[1 skein]
Yellow	⊠ = 740		[0.5 skein]
	◇ = 444		[1 skein]
	• = 445		[1 skein]
Flame red	◉ = 606		[1 skein]

Thread: D.M.C. 6-strand embroidery floss No. 25. See
the arrow for colors and amount.
Finished Size: 29cm by 38cm.
Directions: Match center of fabric and design, and
cross-stitch. Mount and frame.

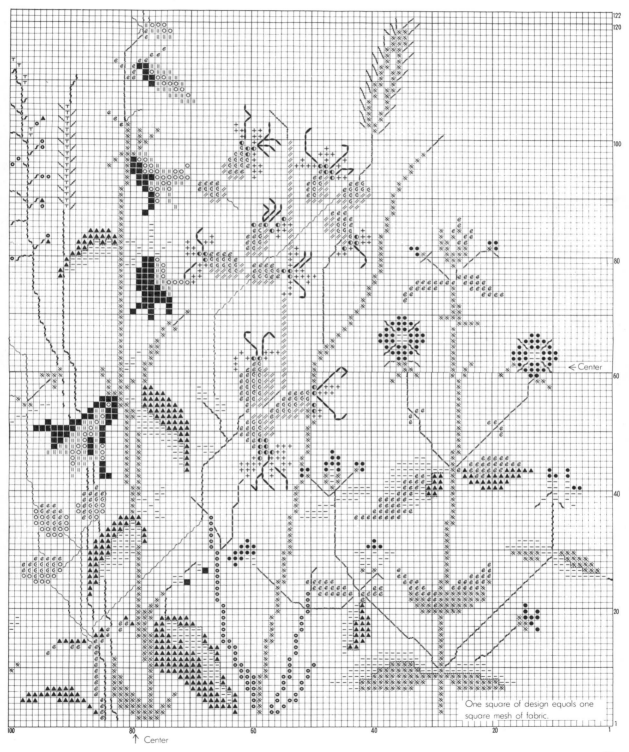

One square of design equals one
square mesh of fabric.

← Center

↑ Center

Materials:

Fabric: Beige Java canvas (35 mesh to 10cm), 45cm by 110cm.

Thread: D.M.C. 6-strand embroidery floss, No. 25. See the arrow for colors and amount.

Finished Size: 35cm by 40cm.

Directions: Match center of fabric and design, and cross-stitch. You may need professional help in finishing the album.

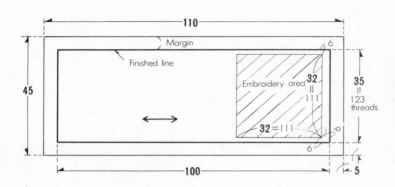

➡ **Color Key** Use 6 strands of floss. Required amount is shown in brackets.

Red

◤ = 902 [1 skein]

✖ = 817 [1 skein]

⊙ = 606 [1 skein]

◇ = 352 [2 skeins]

Ⅰ = 754 [1 skein]

Yellow

◨ = 741 [1 skein]

Z = 725 [2 skeins]

○ = 727 [1 skein]

Blue

■ = 797 [1 skein]

6 = 799 [1 skein]

▽ = 519 [1 skein]

Gray

▲ = 924 [1 skein]

✄ = 926 [1 skein]

∩ = 927 [1 skein]

− = 928 [1 skein]

Green

● = 937 [1 skein]

L = 470 [2 skeins]

/ = 472 [1 skein]

+ = 987 [2 skeins]

S = 368 [2 skeins]

Golden yellow ◉ = 780 [1 skein]

White • = 2 skeins]

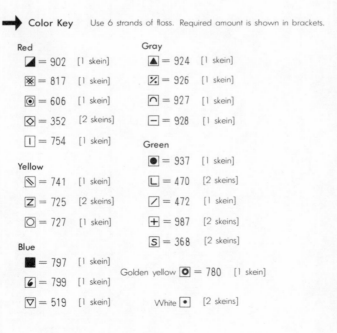

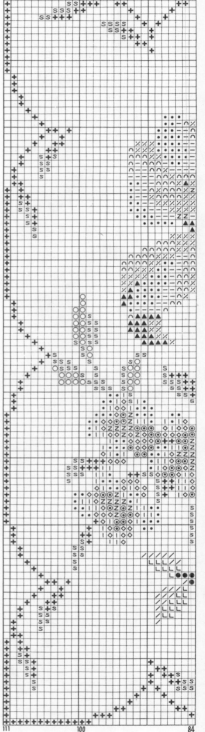

One square of design equals one square mesh of fabric.

Center

Primrose Album Cover *shown on page 17.*

Materials:
Fabric: Beige Indian cloth (52 mesh to 10cm), 44.5cm by 95cm.
Thread: D.M.C. 6-strand embroidery floss, No. 25. See the arrow for colors and amount.
Finished Size: 34.5cm by 40cm.
Directions: Match center of fabric and design, and cross-stitch. You may need professional help in finishing the album.

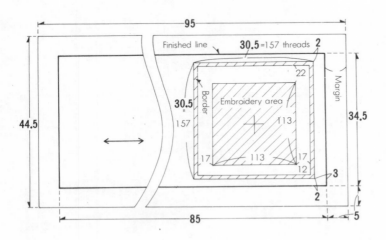

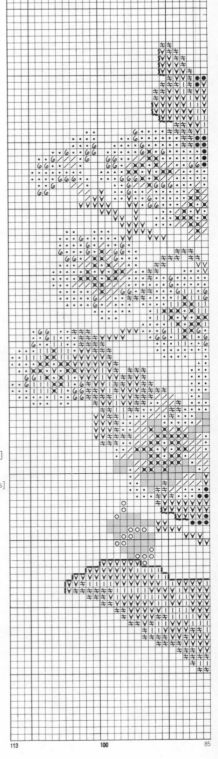

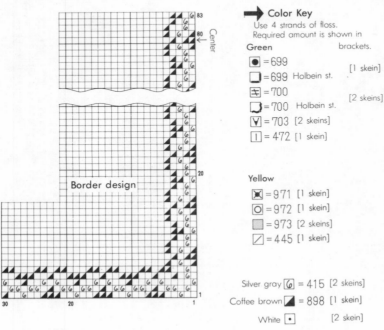

Border design

Color Key

Use 4 strands of floss.
Required amount is shown in brackets.

Green

● = 699		[1 skein]
□ = 699 Holbein st.		
✶ = 700		[2 skeins]
◡ = 700 Holbein st.		
V = 703	[2 skeins]	
I = 472	[1 skein]	

Yellow

✖ = 971	[1 skein]
○ = 972	[1 skein]
▨ = 973	[2 skeins]
╱ = 445	[1 skein]

Silver gray ◖ = 415 [2 skeins]

Coffee brown ◣ = 898 [1 skein]

White • [2 skein]

64

One square of design equals one square mesh of fabric.

Leaf Pochette *shown on page 17.*

Materials:

Fabric: Beige linen (130 mesh to 10cm), 13.5cm square. Brown velveteen, 89cm by 31cm. Cotton fabric for lining, 50cm by 15cm.

Thread: D.M.C. 6-strand embroidery floss, No. 25. See the arrow for colors and amount.

Notions: Golden brown braid, 40cm long. Velcro, 2.5cm.

Finished Size: 20cm by 22cm.

Directions: 1. Cut linen, velveteen and cotton fabric as indicated adding seam allowance.

2. Match centers of linen and design, and cross-stitch.

Turn in seam allowance and sew onto front of pochette. Sew on braid along edge overlapping 0.5cm.

3. With right sides together, sew outer piece and facing.

4. Sew darts of velveteen and cotton fabric respectively.

5. With right sides together, sew front and back pieces respectively. Turn inside out.

6. Insert cotton bag into velveteen with wrong sides facing. Turn in seam allowance and sew facing to lining in slip stitch.

7. Sew on shoulder strap and tassels as shown.

8. Cut Velcro into circle and sew on in place.

Cutting layout of velveteen

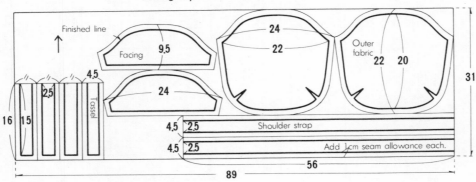

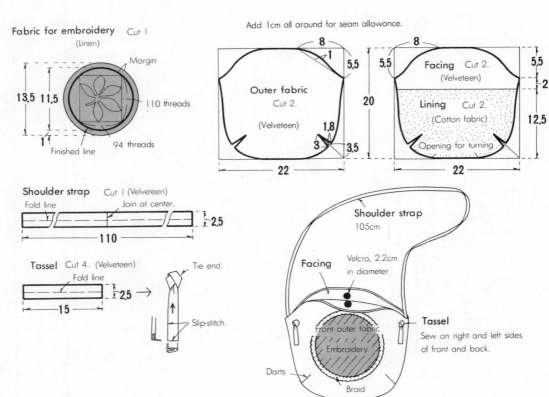

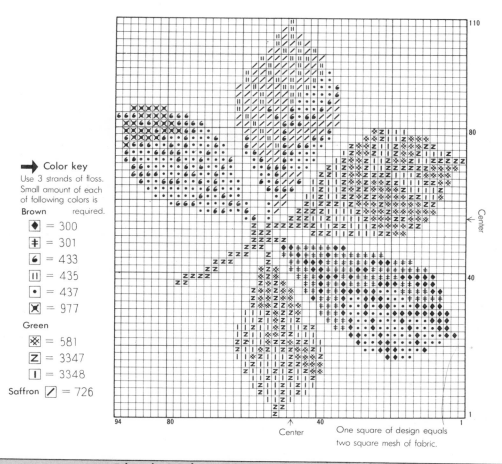

Color key

Use 3 strands of floss. Small amount of each of following colors is required.

Brown
◆ = 300
‡ = 301
6 = 433
II = 435
• = 437
✕ = 977

Green
⊠ = 581
Z = 3347
I = 3348

Saffron ╱ = 726

110

80

Center →

40

1

94   80   40   1

↑
Center

One square of design equals two square mesh of fabric.

Black Velvet Bag *shown on page 16.*

Materials:
Fabric: Black velvet, 50cm by 31cm. Bemberg for lining, 50cm by 31cm. Penelope (or cross-stitch) canvas (60 mesh to 10cm), 12cm square.
Thread: D.M.C. 6-strand embroidery floss, No. 25. See the arrow for colors and amount. Small amount of gold metallic thread for Japanese embroidery.
Notions: Threaded sequins, 0.5cm in diameter and

50cm long. Black rayon cord, 0.6cm in diameter and 200cm long.
Finished Size: 22cm by 28cm.
Directions: Baste Penelope canvas onto embroidery area of velvet. Embroider. Sew on sequins around embroidered area. Make up for bag as shown on next page.

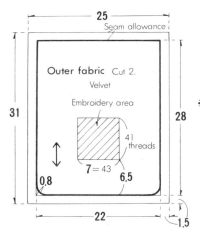

25
Seam allowance
Outer fabric Cut 2.
Velvet
Embroidery area
31
28
41 threads
7 = 43
0.8
6.5
22
1.5

※ **How to cross-stitch on non-mesh fabric**

Use Penelope (or cross-stitch) canvas. Baste canvas onto embroidery area of the fabric and cross-stitch over the canvas and through the fabric. After completing embroidery, remove basting and draw out threads of the canvas, one at a time.

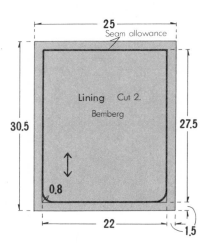

25
Seam allowance
Lining Cut 2.
Bemberg
30.5
27.5
0.8
22
1.5

67

How to make up

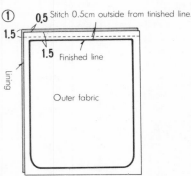

① ⌐0.5 Stitch 0.5cm outside from finished line.

1.5
1.5 Finished line

Outer fabric

Lining

With right sides of velvet and Bemberg together, sew top edge. Repeat for back piece.

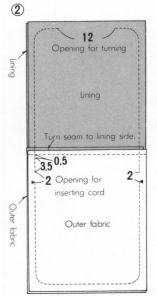

②
Lining

⌐12⌐ Opening for turning

Lining

Turn seam to lining side.

3.5 0.5
2 Opening for inserting cord
2

Outer fabric

Outer fabric

With right sides together, sew side and bottom seams of front and back pieces, catching tassels at ▲-marked places and leaving bottom of lining open for turning. Turn to right side. Slip-stitch opening closed.

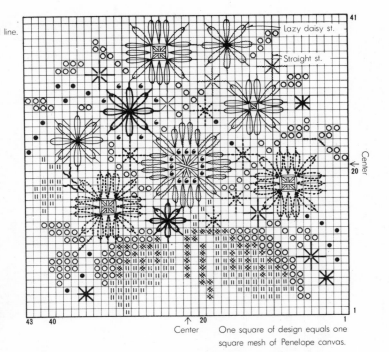

41

Lazy daisy st.

Straight st.

Center
20

43 40   ↑ 20   1
      Center   One square of design equals one square mesh of Penelope canvas.

Use 4 strands of floss unless otherwise indicated.

➡ **Color and Stitch Key** Small amount of each of following colors is required.

		Cross-st.	Holbein st.	Double cross-st.		Lazy daisy st.	Straight st.	Four-sided st. (Page 36.)
Purple	209	6				⬭	- - - -	
	553		◲			⬭	—	
	554		◲			⬭	～～～	
Green	470	�II						
	907	◎	◲					
Yellow	444	⊠		⊞	✳			⊞
Brown	780	⊠						
Gold metallic thread, with 2 strands		⊙		✳		⬭		

③
0.5
Lining

3.5
2

Opening for inserting cord

Stitch for casing with right side facing.

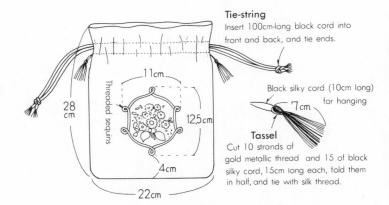

Threaded sequins

28 cm

11cm
12.5 cm
4cm
22cm

Tie-string
Insert 100cm-long black cord into front and back, and tie ends.

Black silky cord (10cm long) for hanging

7cm

Tassel
Cut 10 strands of gold metallic thread and 15 of black silky cord, 15cm long each, fold them in half, and tie with silk thread.

68

Coasters *shown on page 20.*

Materials (for one):
Fabric: Indian cloth (52 mesh to 10cm); beige, pink, and blue, 12cm square each. Cotton broadcloth, 12cm square.
Thread: D.M.C. 6-strand embroidery floss, No. 25. See the arrow for colors and amount.
Notions: Lace edging, 35cm long.

Finished Size: 11cm in diameter (including lace edging).
Directions: Match centers of fabric and design, and cross-stitch. With right sides facing, sew front and back (lining) together with lace edging in between, leaving 5cm open for turning. Turn inside out. Slip-stitch opening closed.

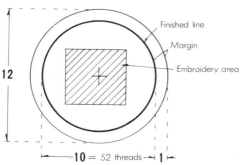

Finished line
Margin
Embroidery area
12
10 = 52 threads 1
Cut cotton broadcloth same size as Indian cloth.

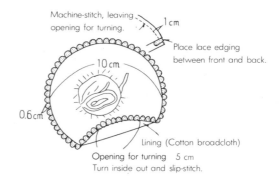

Machine-stitch, leaving opening for turning.
1 cm
Place lace edging between front and back.
10 cm
0.6 cm
Lining (Cotton broadcloth)
Opening for turning 5 cm
Turn inside out and slip-stitch.

Chestnut Coaster

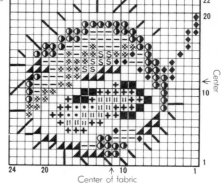

Color Key Use 4 strands of floss unless otherwise indicated.
Small amount of each of following colors is required for one coaster.

Brown
■ = 300
+ = 301
※ = 435
‖ = 437
◆ = 433
— = 433
Straight st. with 2 strands.

Green
◢ = 3345
S = 3347
– = 3348
◐ = 581

Saffron
• = 726

Leaf Coaster

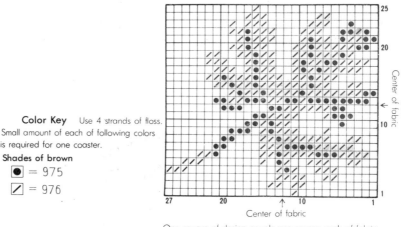

Color Key Use 4 strands of floss.
Small amount of each of following colors is required for one coaster.

Shades of brown
● = 975
╱ = 976

One square of design equals one square mesh of fabric.

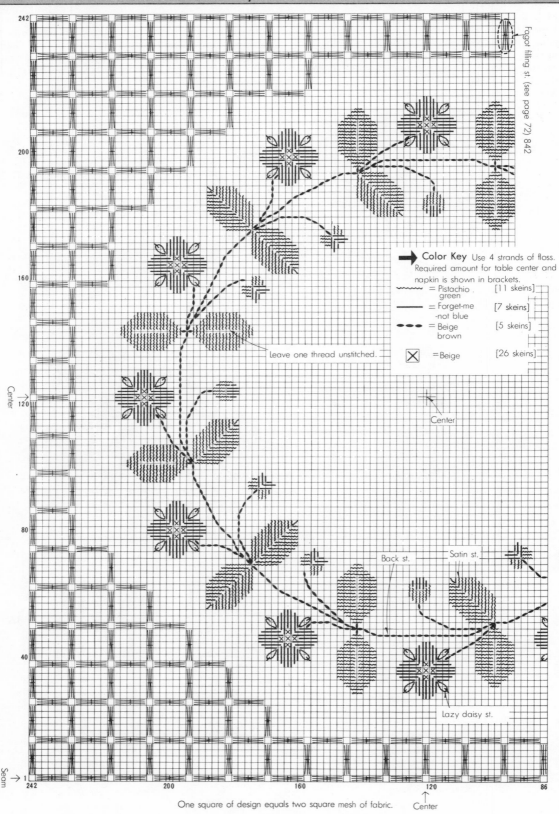

Fagot filling st. (see page 72) 842

Color Key Use 4 strands of floss.
Required amount for table center and
napkin is shown in brackets.

≈ = Pistachio green [11 skeins]

— = Forget-me-not blue [7 skeins]

•--• = Beige brown [5 skeins]

☒ = Beige [26 skeins]

Leave one thread unstitched.

Center

Center

Back st.

Satin st.

Lazy daisy st.

Center

Seam

One square of design equals two square mesh of fabric.

Center

70

Materials:
Fabric: Beige Oxford cloth (79 mesh to 10cm); 90cm by 370cm for Table Center: 91cm square for 4 napkins.
Thread: D.M.C. 6-strand embroidery floss, No. 25. See the arrow for colors and amount.
Finished Size: Table Center, 125cm by 170cm. Napkin, 39.5cm square.
Directions: For Table Center: Sew pieces of fabric to get designated size. Match center of fabric and design, and embroider. Draw out 4 threads crosswise and lengthwise from fabric, turn edges back twice and hem, mitering corners.
For Napkin: Embroider as indicated. Draw out 2 threads crosswise and lengthwise from fabric. Turn edges back twice and hem, mitering corners.

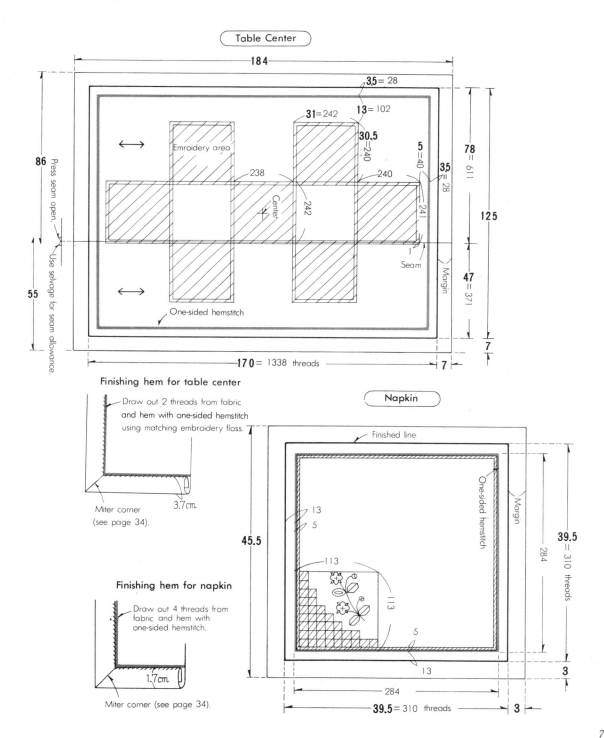

Table Center

184

3.5 = 28
31 = 242   13 = 102
30.5 = 240
Emroidery area
5 = 40
78 = 611
238   240
3.5 = 28
86
Press seam open.   Center
242   241
125
Use selvage for seam allowance.   1
Seam
Margin
47 = 371
55
One-sided hemstitch
7
170 = 1338 threads   7

Finishing hem for table center

Draw out 2 threads from fabric and hem with one-sided hemstitch using matching embroidery floss.

Miter corner (see page 34).   3.7cm

Napkin

Finished line

45.5
One-sided hemstitch
Margin
39.5 = 310 threads
13
5
284
113
113
5
3
13
284
39.5 = 310 threads   3

Finishing hem for napkin

Draw out 4 threads from fabric and hem with one-sided hemstitch.

Miter corner (see page 34).   1.7cm

71

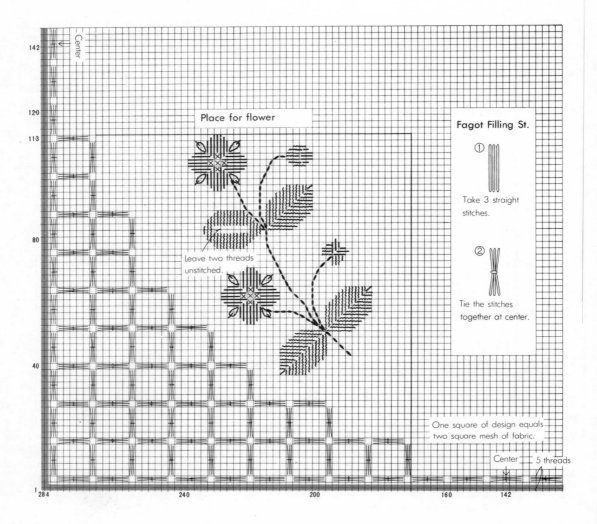

Place for flower

Leave two threads unstitched.

Fagot Filling St.

① Take 3 straight stitches.

② Tie the stitches together at center.

One square of design equals two square mesh of fabric.

Center ⊥ 5 threads

Materials:

Fabric: Blue Java canvas (35 mesh to 10cm), 39.5cm square.

Thread: D.M.C. 6-strand embroidery floss, No. 25. See the arrow for colors and amount.

Notions: Blue braid, 125cm long.

Finished Size: 37.5cm in diameter.

Directions: Match center of fabric and design, and cross-stitch. Turn edge toward center from finished line, place braid along edge and machine-stitch.

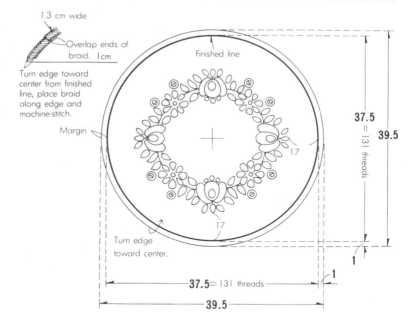

1.3 cm wide

Overlap ends of braid. 1cm

Turn edge toward center from finished line, place braid along edge and machine-stitch.

Finished line

Margin

Turn edge toward center.

17

17

37.5 = 131 threads

39.5

37.5 = 131 threads

39.5

1

1

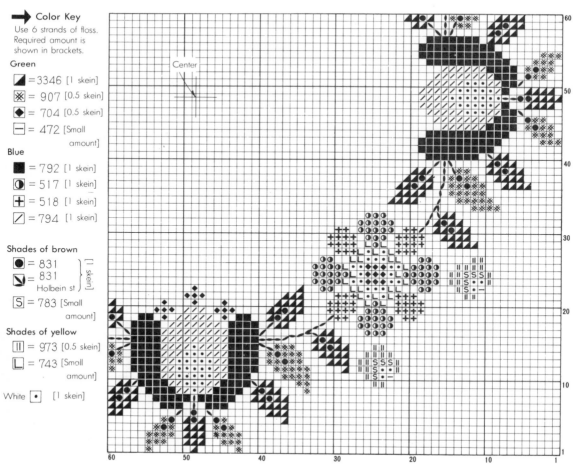

Color Key

Use 6 strands of floss. Required amount is shown in brackets.

Green

◩ = 3346 [1 skein]

✖ = 907 [0.5 skein]

◆ = 704 [0.5 skein]

⊟ = 472 [Small amount]

Blue

◼ = 792 [1 skein]

◑ = 517 [1 skein]

✚ = 518 [1 skein]

╱ = 794 [1 skein]

Shades of brown

● = 831 ⎫ [1 skein]
◪ = 831 ⎬
  Holbein st ⎭

S = 783 [Small amount]

Shades of yellow

‖ = 973 [0.5 skein]

L = 743 [Small amount]

White • [1 skein]

Center

One square of design equals one square mesh of fabric.

Materials:
Fabric: Beige Java canvas (35 mesh to 10cm), 42cm square.
Thread: D.M.C. 6-strand embroidery floss, No. 25. See the arrow for colors and amount.
Finished Size: 34cm square.
Directions: Match center of fabric and design, and cross-stich. Turn edges back twice and slip-stitch, mitering corners.

Finishing hem

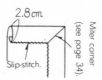

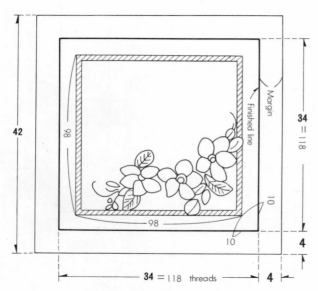

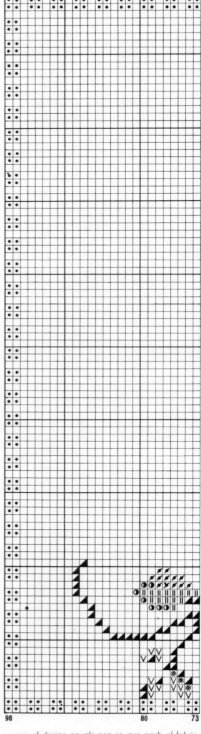

One square of design equals one square mesh of fabric.

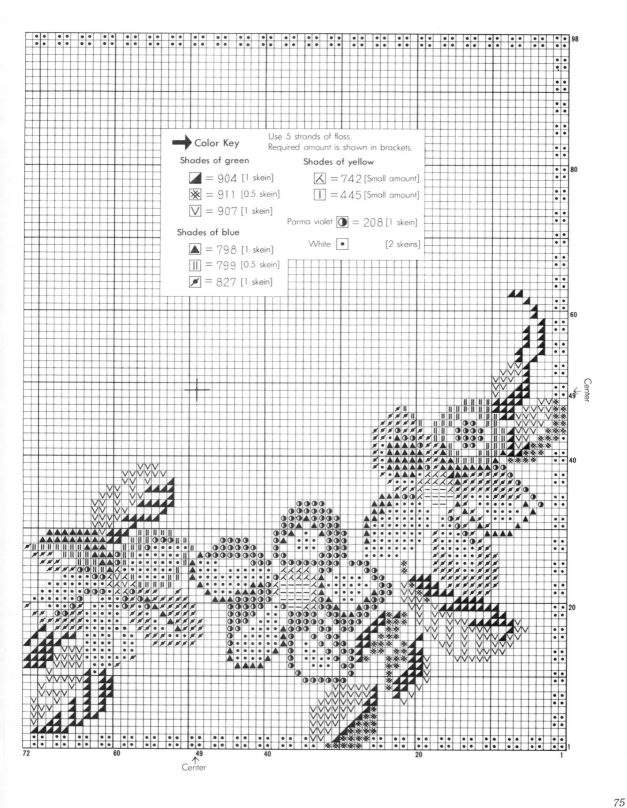

Color Key

Use 5 strands of floss.
Required amount is shown in brackets.

Shades of green

◩ = 904 [1 skein]
✖ = 911 [0.5 skein]
V = 907 [1 skein]

Shades of blue

▲ = 798 [1 skein]
‖ = 799 [0.5 skein]
◪ = 827 [1 skein]

Shades of yellow

⋏ = 742 [Small amount]
I = 445 [Small amount]

Parma violet ◖ = 208 [1 skein]

White • [2 skeins]

Materials:
Fabric: Beige linen (130 mesh to 10cm), 21cm square.
Thread: D.M.C. 6-strand embroidery floss, No. 25. See the arrow for colors and amount.
Finished Size: 11cm square.
Directions: Match center of fabric and design, and cross-stitch. Mount and frame.

Stitch and Color Key
Use 3 strands of floss.
Required amount is shown in brackets.

		Cross st.	Half-cross st.	Holbein st.	
Black	310	■	▨	◪	[0.5 skein]
Shades of brown	3371	◣			[Small amount]
	839	◪		▢	[Small amount]
	434	⊠	⊠		[0.5 skein]
Shades of green	936	∨			[0.5 skein]
	732	ℓ			[0.5 skein]
	734	S			[0.5 skein]
Red	498	⊠	⊠		[0.5 skein]
	326	◎	⊘		[0.5 skein]
Tangerine yellow	741	⊠	⊠		[0.5 skein]
	743	◎			[Small amount]
Blue	792	▥			[Small amount]
	517	⊞	⊞		[Small amount]
Ash gray	317	◭			[Small amount]
	318	△	△		[0.5 skein]
White		·			[0.5 skein]
Episcopal purple	915	⊠			[0.5 skein]
Parma violet	211			▨	[Small amount]

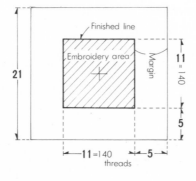

Finished line
Embroidery area
Margin
21
11 = 140
5
11 = 140   5
threads

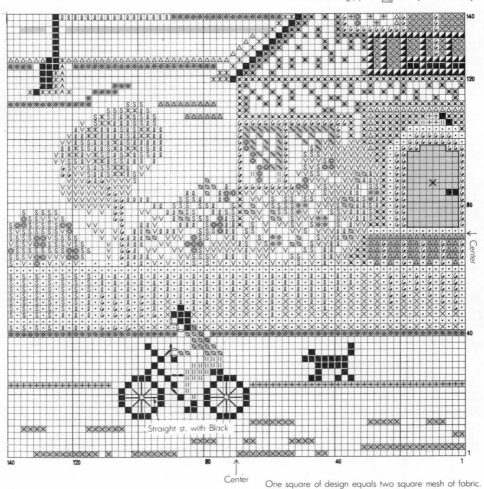

Straight st. with Black

← Center

One square of design equals two square mesh of fabric.

↑
Center

Small Picture (Sailboat) *shown on page 22.*

Materials:

Fabric: Beige linen (130 mesh to 10cm), 25cm square.

Thread: D.M.C. 6-strand embroidery floss, No. 25. See the arrow for colors and amount.

Finished Size: 15cm square.

Directions: Match center of fabric and design, and cross-stitch. Mount and frame.

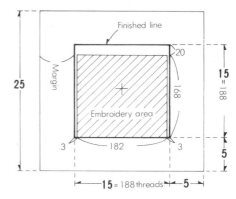

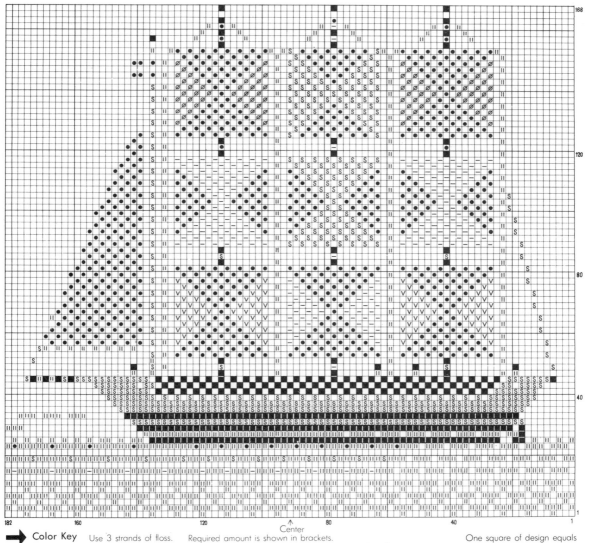

➡ **Color Key** Use 3 strands of floss. Required amount is shown in brackets.

One square of design equals two square mesh of fabric.

Shades of blue
Ø = 791 [0.5 skein]
‖ = 798 [1 skein]

Garnet red
● = 326 [1 skein]

Black
■ = 310 [0.5 skein]

Plum
S = 553 [0.5 skein]

Tangerine yellow
V = 742 [0.5 skein]

Parakeet green
— = 906 [0.5 skein]

Materials:

Fabric: Beige linen (130 mesh to 10cm), 22cm square.

Thread: D.M.C. 6-strand embroidery floss, No. 25. See the arrow for colors and amount.

Finished Size: 12cm square.

Directions: Match center of fabric and design, and cross-stitch. Mount and frame.

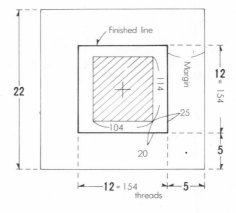

Color Key

Use 3 strands of floss.
Small amount of each of following colors is requried.

Yellow

$\boxed{\cdot}$ = 744

$\left.\begin{array}{l} \boxed{Z} \\ \text{Lazy daisy st.} \end{array}\right\}$ = 972

$\boxed{\varnothing}$ = 971

Shades of brown

$\left.\begin{array}{l} \boxed{\bullet} \\ \text{Holbein st.} \end{array}\right\}$ = 782

$\left.\begin{array}{l} \blacksquare \\ \text{Outline st.} \end{array}\right\}$ = 3031

Shades of green

$\boxed{\diagdown}$ = 906

$\boxed{\times}$ = 580

Shades of red

$\boxed{-}$ = 350

$\boxed{\times}$ = 816

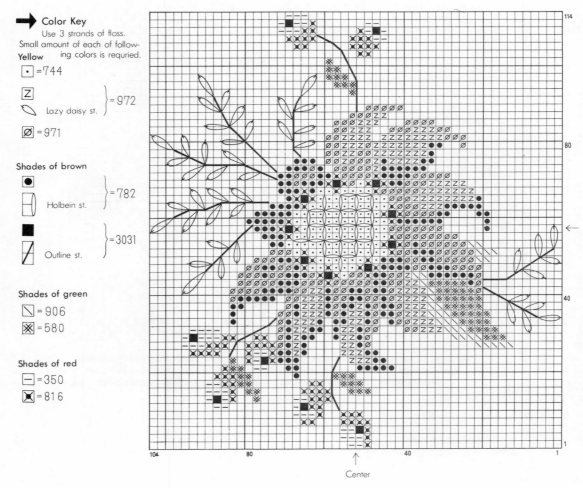

Center

One square of design equals two square mesh of fabric.

Materials:

Fabric: Beige Java canvas (41 mesh to 10cm), 25cm square.

Thread: D.M.C. 6-strand embroidery floss, No. 25. See the arrow for colors and amount.

Finished Size: 22cm square.

Directions: Match center of fabric and design, and cross-stitch. Mount and frame.

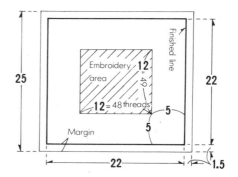

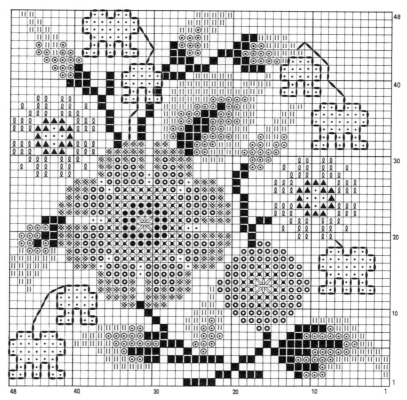

One square of design equals one square mesh of fabric.

➡ Color Key Use 6 strands of floss unless otherwise indicated. Required amount is shown in brackets.

Green

■ = 3345 [Small amount]

⊙ = 905 [Small amount]

‖ = 703
╱ = 703 } [1 skein]
Holbein st. with 3 strands

Purple

● = 550 [Small amount]

❇ = 553 [Small amount]

Peony red

✖ = 718 [Small amount]

⊙ = 603 [Small amount]

Blue

▲ = 806 [Small amount]

ℓ = 807 [Small amount]

· Cross st.
Double cross st. } White [Small amount]

Materials:
Fabric: Beige Java canvas (35 mesh to 10cm), 41cm square.
Thread: D.M.C. 6-strand embroidery floss, No. 25. See the arrow for colors and amount.
Finished Size: 33cm square.
Directions: Match center of fabric and design, and cross-stitch. Turn edges back twice and slip-stitch, mitering corners.

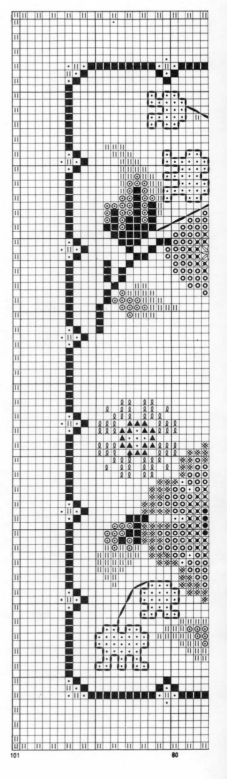

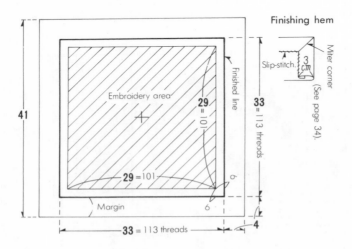

Finishing hem

Slip-stitch.

Miter corner
(See page 34).

Color Key Use 6 strands of floss unless otherwise indicated.
Required amount is shown in brackets.

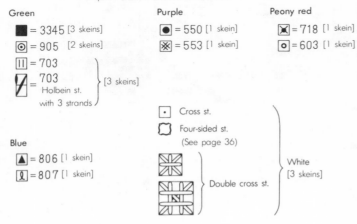

Green

■ = 3345 [3 skeins]
◉ = 905 [2 skeins]
‖ = 703
⧄ = 703 Holbein st. with 3 strands } [3 skeins]

Blue

▲ = 806 [1 skein]
⚉ = 807 [1 skein]

Purple

● = 550 [1 skein]
✕ = 553 [1 skein]

Peony red

⊠ = 718 [1 skein]
▣ = 603 [1 skein]

• Cross st.
▢ Four-sided st. (See page 36)
✕ Double cross st.

White [3 skeins]

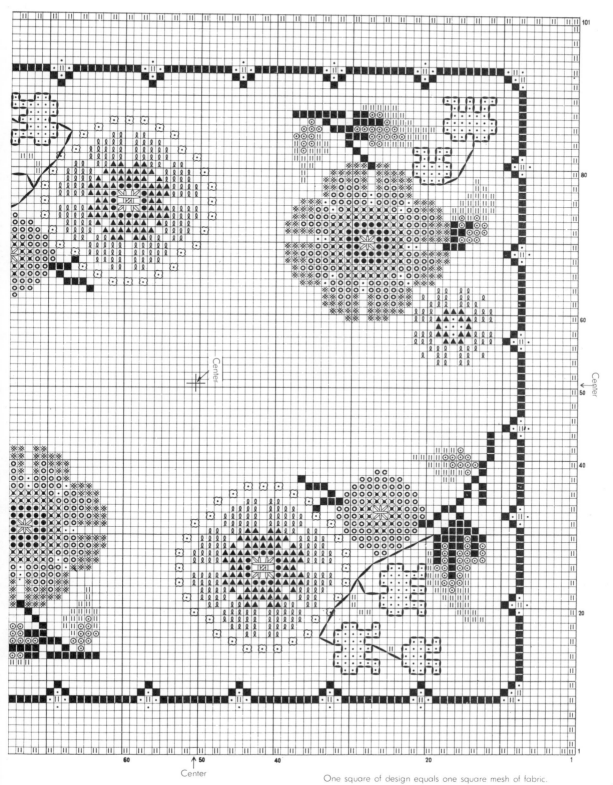

One square of design equals one square mesh of fabric.

Bluebird and Flower Runner *shown on page 24.*

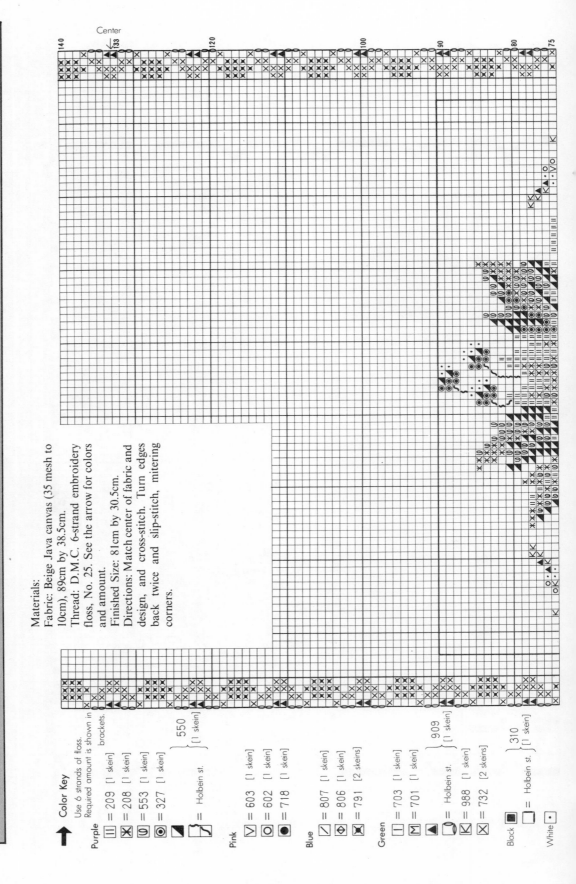

Materials:
Fabric: Beige Java canvas (35 mesh to 10cm), 89cm by 38.5cm.
Thread: D.M.C. 6-strand embroidery floss, No. 25. See the arrow for colors and amount.
Finished Size: 81cm by 30.5cm.
Directions: Match center of fabric and design, and cross-stitch. Turn edges back twice and slip-stitch, mitering corners.

▲ **Color Key**

Use 6 strands of floss.
Required amount is shown in brackets.

Purple
⫴ = 209 [1 skein]
✕ = 208 [1 skein]
Ⓤ = 553 [1 skein]
◉ = 327 [1 skein]
◣ = 550 [1 skein]
〜 = Holbein st. [1 skein]

Pink
⋁ = 603 [1 skein]
◯ = 602 [1 skein]
⊠ = 718 [2 skeins]

Blue
◿ = 807 [1 skein]
◈ = 806 [1 skein]
⊠ = 791 [2 skeins]

Green
⫴ = 703 [1 skein]
Ⓜ = 701 [1 skein]
◀ = 909 Holbein st. [1 skein]
Ⓞ = 988 [1 skein]
Ⓚ = 732 [2 skeins]
✕ = 310 [1 skein]

Black
■ = Holbein st. [1 skein]

White
· =

82

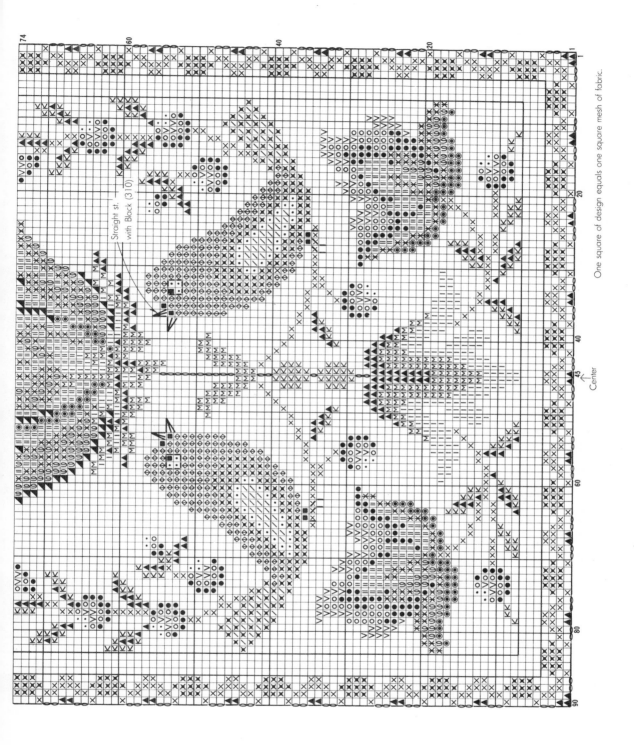

Straight st.
with Black (310)

One square of design equals one square mesh of fabric.

Center

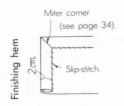

Finishing hem

Miter corner
(see page 34).

2cm

Slip-stitch.

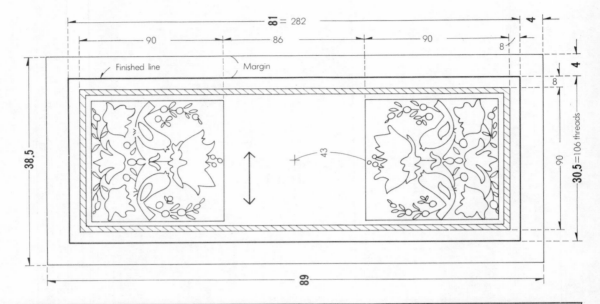

Small Pillows *shown on page 26.*

Materials (for one):
Fabric: Java canvas (41 mesh to 10cm); natural, pink and blue, 64cm by 32cm each.
Thread: D.M.C. 6-strand embroidery floss, No. 25. See the arrow for colors and amount.
Notions: Inner pillow, 30cm square, stuffed with 180g of kapok. Lavender cotton cord, 0.5cm in diameter and 135cm long.

Finished Size: 29cm square.
Directions: Match centers of fabric and design, and cross-stitch. Sew front and back pieces together with right sides facing, leaving opening for turning. Turn inside out. Insert inner pillow and slip-stitch opening closed. Sew on cotton cord all around.

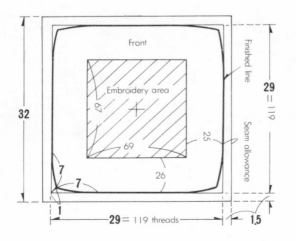

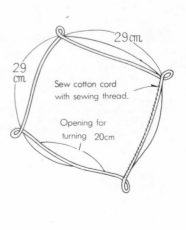

※ Cut back piece same size as front.

One square of design equals one square mesh of fabric.

Color Key Use 5 strands of floss. Required amount is shown in brackets.

Shades of purple

⊠ = 327 ⎫
⬒ = 327 Holbein st. ⎬ [0.5 skein]
𝟨 = 208 [1 skein]
ℓ = 554 [1 skein]

Shades of green

▲ = 991 ⎫
⬒ = 991 Holbein st. ⎬ [0.5 skein]
✕ = 701 [0.5 skein]
‖ = 703 [1 skein]

Shades of blue

◆ = 792 [0.5 skein]
◎ = 798 [0.5 skein]
S = 996 [0.5 skein]

Geranium red ● = 817 [0.5 skein]
Cerise Z = 601 [0.5 skein]
Canary yellow O = 971 [0.5 skein]
White • [0.5 skein]

85

Bluebird and Flower Table Center *shown on page 25.*

Materials:

Fabric: White Java canvas (41 mesh to 10cm), 46cm square.

Thread: D.M.C. 6-strand embroidery floss, No. 25. See the arrow for colors and amount.

Notions: Lace edging, 150cm long. Bias tape, 0.7cm wide and 150cm long.

Finished Size: 48cm in diameter (including lace edging).

Directions: Match center of fabric and design, and cross-stitch. Sew lace edging all around with bias tape.

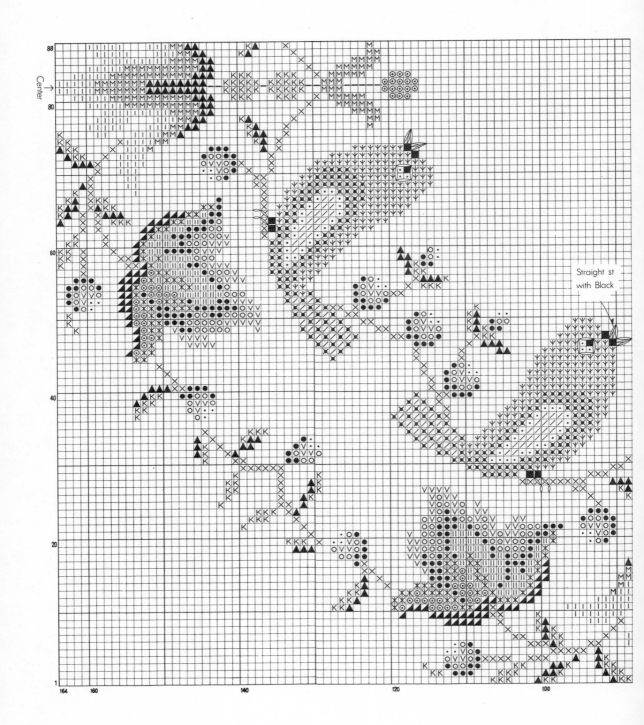

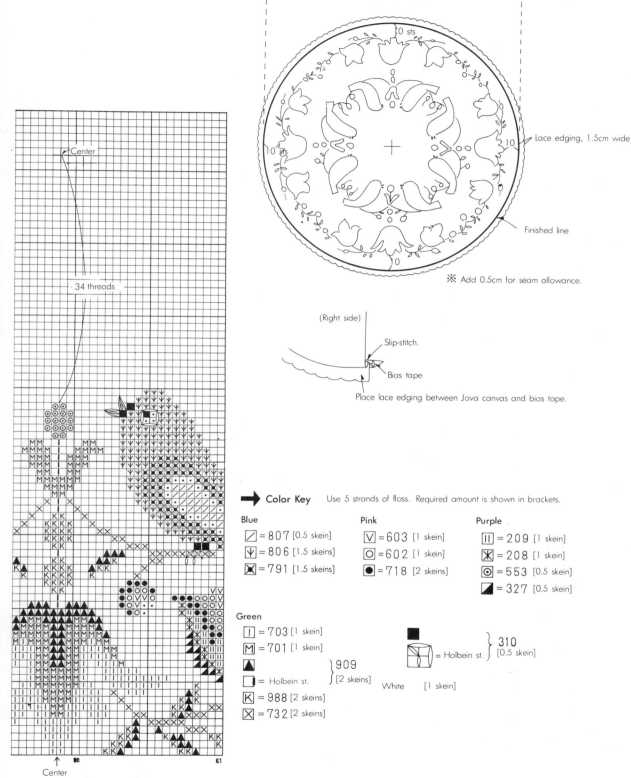

45 = 184 threads

10 sts

Lace edging, 1.5cm wide

Finished line

10 sts

10

0

0

※ Add 0.5cm for seam allowance.

(Right side)

Slip-stitch.

Bias tape

Place lace edging between Java canvas and bias tape.

Center

34 threads

Center

80

61

One square of design equals one square mesh of fabric.

Color Key   Use 5 strands of floss. Required amount is shown in brackets.

Blue
◹ = 807 [0.5 skein]
↓ = 806 [1.5 skeins]
⊠ = 791 [1.5 skeins]

Pink
V = 603 [1 skein]
O = 602 [1 skein]
● = 718 [2 skeins]

Purple
|| = 209 [1 skein]
⊠ = 208 [1 skein]
◉ = 553 [0.5 skein]
◪ = 327 [0.5 skein]

Green
| = 703 [1 skein]
M = 701 [1 skein]
▲ }
□ = Holbein st. } 909 [2 skeins]
K = 988 [2 skeins]
X = 732 [2 skeins]

■
⊡ = Holbein st. } 310 [0.5 skein]

White   [1 skein]

Materials (for one):

Fabric: Beige Java canvas (35 mesh to 10cm), 82cm by 39.5cm.

Thread: D.M.C. 6-strand embroidery floss, No. 25. See the arrow for colors and amount.

Notions: Inner pillow, 38cm square, stuffed with 300g of kapok. Zipper, 25cm long.

Finished Size: 35.5cm square.

Directions: Match center of fabric and design, and cross-stitch. Sew zipper onto back pieces. Sew front and back pieces together with right sides facing. Turn inside out. Insert inner pillow.

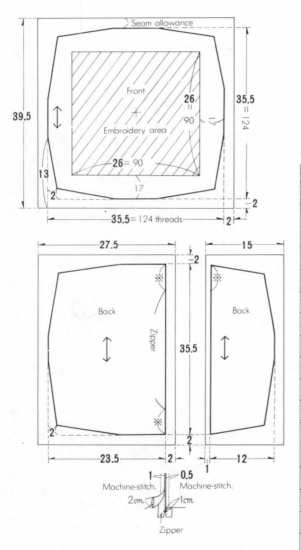

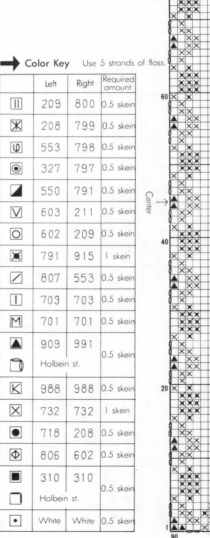

Color Key Use 5 strands of floss.

	Left	Right	Required amount
‖	209	800	0.5 skein
✳	208	799	0.5 skein
Ⓤ	553	798	0.5 skein
⊙	327	797	0.5 skein
◢	550	791	0.5 skein
V	603	211	0.5 skein
O	602	209	0.5 skein
✖	791	915	1 skein
╱	807	553	0.5 skein
I	703	703	0.5 skein
M	701	701	0.5 skein
▲	909	991	0.5 skein
▯ Holbein st.			
K	988	988	0.5 skein
✕	732	732	1 skein
●	718	208	0.5 skein
◈	806	602	0.5 skein
▪	310	310	0.5 skein
▢ Holbein st.			
⊡	White	White	0.5 skein

Straight st.
with Black (310)

One square of design equals one square mesh of fabric.

Pochette *shown on page 27.*

Materials:
Fabric: Pink Indian cloth (52 mesh to 10cm), 47cm by 21cm. Cotton broadcloth for lining, 33cm by 100cm.

Thread: D.M.C. 6-strand embroidery floss, No. 25. See the arrow for colors and amount.

Notions: Velcro, 3cm.
Finished Size: 17.5cm deep and 21cm wide.
Directions: Match centers of front and design, and cross-stitch. Make pochette following diagrams below.

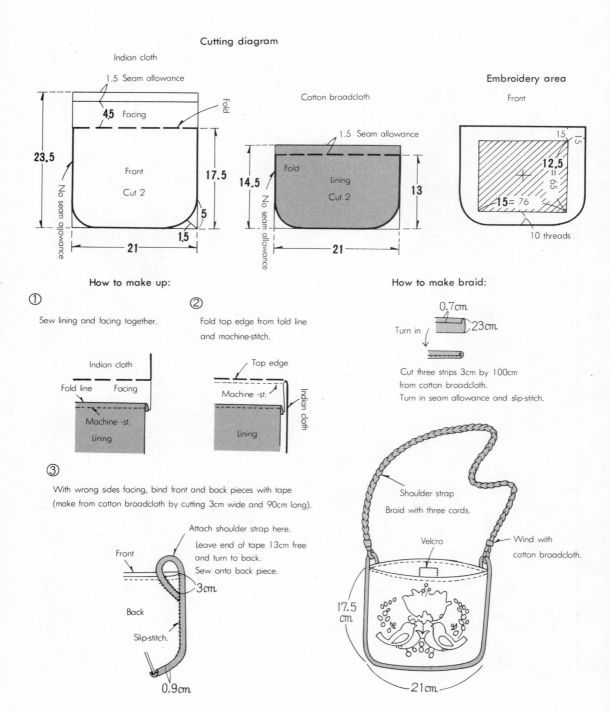

Cutting diagram

Indian cloth

1.5 Seam allowance

4.5 Facing

Fold

23.5

Front
Cut 2

No seam allowance

17.5

5

1.5

21

Cotton broadcloth

1.5 Seam allowance

Fold

Lining
Cut 2

14.5

No seam allowance

13

21

Embroidery area

Front

15

15

12.5 = 65

15 = 76

10 threads

How to make up:

① Sew lining and facing together.

Indian cloth

Fold line   Facing

Machine-st.
Lining

② Fold top edge from fold line and machine-stitch.

Top edge

Machine-st.

Lining

Indian cloth

③ With wrong sides facing, bind front and back pieces with tape (make from cotton broadcloth by cutting 3cm wide and 90cm long).

Attach shoulder strap here.
Leave end of tape 13cm free and turn to back.
Sew onto back piece.

Front

Back

Slip-stitch.

3cm

0.9cm

How to make braid:

0.7cm

Turn in

23cm

Cut three strips 3cm by 100cm from cotton broadcloth.
Turn in seam allowance and slip-stitch.

Shoulder strap
Braid with three cords.

Velcro

Wind with cotton broadcloth.

17.5 cm

21cm

90

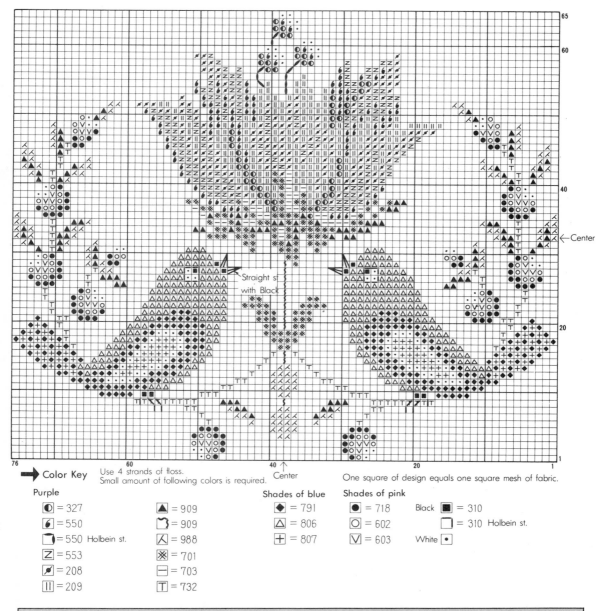

➡ **Color Key**   Use 4 strands of floss.
Small amount of following colors is required.   Center   One square of design equals one square mesh of fabric.

Purple

◑ = 327		▲ = 909	
𝟨 = 550		◻ = 909	
◻ = 550 Holbein st.		人 = 988	
Ƶ = 553		✖ = 701	
✐ = 208		⊟ = 703	
Ⅲ = 209		T = 732	

Shades of blue

◆ = 791
△ = 806
+ = 807

Shades of pink

● = 718   Black ■ = 310
○ = 602   ◻ = 310 Holbein st.
V = 603   White •

Pincushions (e) and (f) shown on page 29.

Materials (for one):

Fabric: Pink (or blue) Indian cloth (52 mesh to 10cm), 26cm by 13cm.

Thread: D.M.C. 6-strand embroidery floss, No. 25. See the arrow for colors and amount.

Notions: Lace edging, 65cm long. Pink (or blue) bias tape, 1.5cm wide and 37 cm long. Scraps of yarn.

Finished Size: 18cm in diameter (including lace edging).

Directions: Match centers of fabric and design and cross-stitch. make pincushion following diagrams on next page.

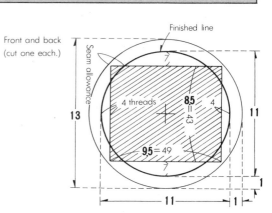

How to make up:

①
Opening for stuffing
5cm
Back
(wrong side)

Wrong side — Lace edging
Lace
Run a gathering stitch and pull thread to gather.
Join ends.

Machine-stitch
Fold.
Yarn

Bias tape
Fold bias tape in half lengthwise, place 2 - 3 strands of yarn, and machine-stitch.

Front
(Right side)

With right sides facing, sew front and back pieces together with lace edging and bias tape in between, leaving opening for stuffing.

②
Back
Opening for stuffing

Turn inside out. stuff with yarn and slip-stitch opening closed.

Lace, 3.5 cm wide.

Bias tape, 0.3cm wide.

—18—

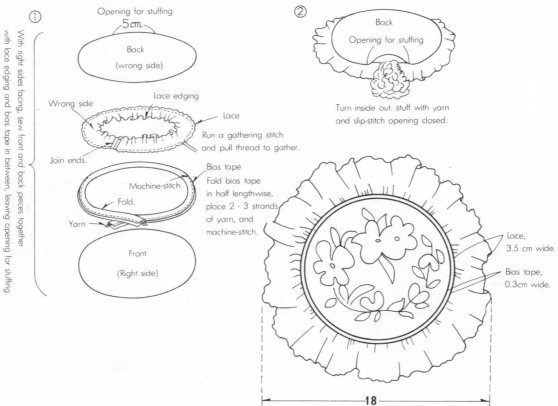

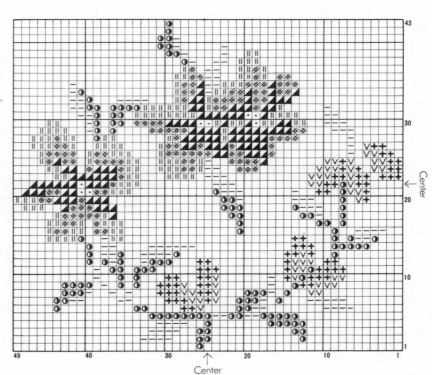

Color Key

Use 3 strands of floss.
Small amlunt of each of following colors is required.

Shades of purple

◪ = 550

※ = 552

‖ = 554

Shades of green

◑ = 905

─ = 907

Shades of pink

✚ = 892

Ⅴ = 894

Canary yellow

• = 973

One square of design equals one square mesh of fabric.

Center

Center

Materials (for one):
Fabric: Beige Indian cloth (52 mesh to 10cm), 28cm by 13cm.
Thread: D.M.C. 6-strand embroidery floss, No. 25. See the arrow for colors and amount,
Notions: Brown (olive green for (b)) cord for piping, 50cm long. Scraps of yarn.

Finished Size: 12 cm by 11cm.
Directions: Match center of fabric and design, and cross-stitch. Sew front and back pieces together with right sides facing and with cord in between, leaving opening for stuffing. Turn inside out. Stuff with yarn scraps and slip-stitch opening closed.

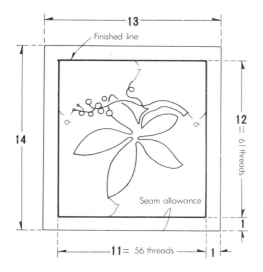

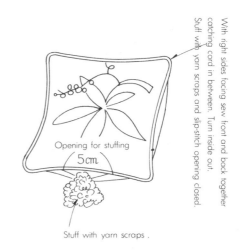

With right sides facing sew front and back together catching cord in between. Turn inside out. Stuff with yarn scraps and slip-stitch opening closed.

Opening for stuffing 5cm.

Stuff with yarn scraps.

※ Cut back piece same size as front.

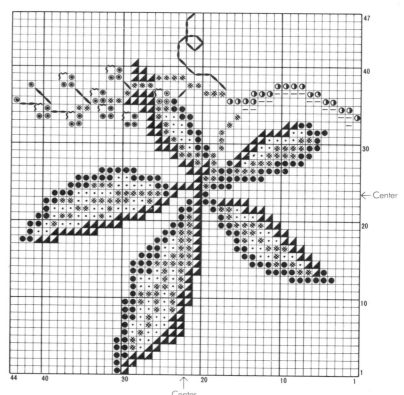

Color Key Use 4 strands of floss. Small amount of each of following colors is required.

	a	b
●	3345	470
⊠ Holbein st. ◣	3347	702
·	3348	704
◐	433	433
−	435	435
◢	347	987
◉ Holbein st.	311	915

One square of design equals one square mesh of fabric.

Materials (for one):
Fabric: Beige Indian cloth (52 mesh to 10cm), 30cm by 16cm.
Thread: D.M.C. 6-strand embroidery floss, No. 25. See the arrow for colors and amount.
Notions: Ribbon, 0.9cm wide and 23cm long. Cotton lace edging, 1.5cm wide and 60cm long. Small amount of cotton.
Finished Size: See diagram.
Directions: Embroider as indicated. Make princushion following diagram.

Actual-size pattern

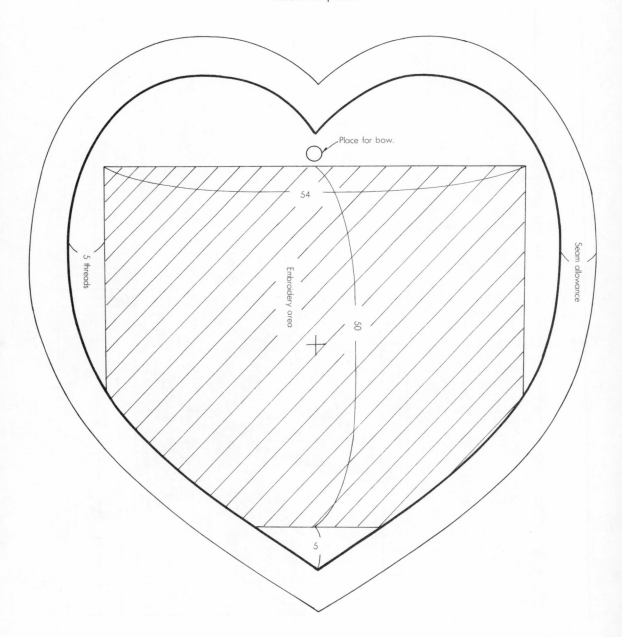

Place for bow.

54

5 threads

Seam allowance

Embroidery area

50

5

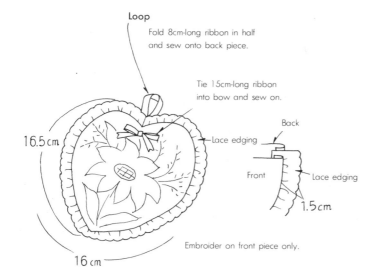

Loop

Fold 8cm-long ribbon in half and sew onto back piece.

Tie 15cm-long ribbon into bow and sew on.

16.5 cm

Lace edging

16 cm

Back

Front

Lace edging

1.5 cm

Embroider on front piece only.

Color Key   Use 4 strands of floss.

Half skein each of following colors is required.

Signs	c	d
╱	906	906
✕	580	580
●	824	3350
◎	826	3687
II	813	3688
⬭ Lazy daisy st.		
·	744	744
N	782	782
▢ Holbein st.		
I	741	741
✕	3031	3031
▢ Holbein st.		

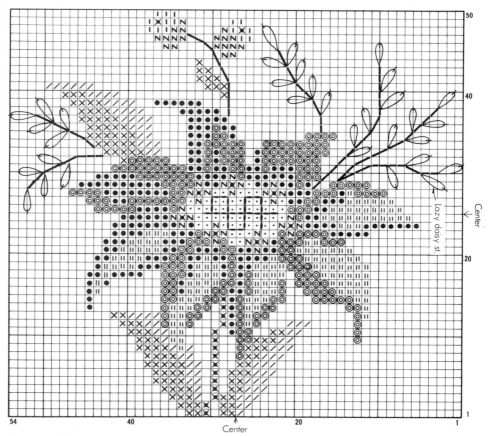

One square of design equals one square mesh of fabric.

Materials:
Fabric: Blue Indian cloth (52 mesh to 10cm), 34cm by 7cm. Bemberg for lining, 34cm by 7cm.
Thread: D.M.C. 6-strand embroidery floss, No. 25. See the arrow for colors and amount.
Notions: Bias tape, 1.6cm wide and 35cm long.
Finished Size: 7cm wide and 15.5cm long.
Directions: Match center of fabric and design, and embroider on front piece. Make scissors case following diagrams.

Actual-size pattern

Indian cloth
Lining } Cut 2 each.

Bias tape

No seam allowance

78 threads

2

2

8

Required length of fabric

Margin

29 threads

Required width of fabric

How to make up:

① Turn in seam allowance of bottom edges and slip-stitch lining to Indian cloth. (Repeat for back piece.)

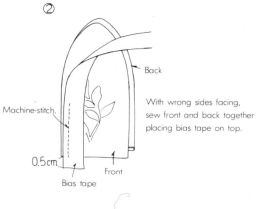

Place lining 0.2 cm inside from Indian cloth.

②

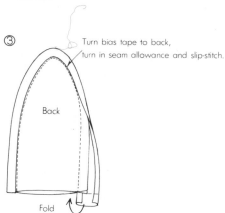

With wrong sides facing, sew front and back together placing bias tape on top.

③ Turn bias tape to back, turn in seam allowance and slip-stitch.

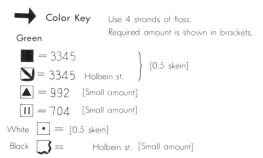

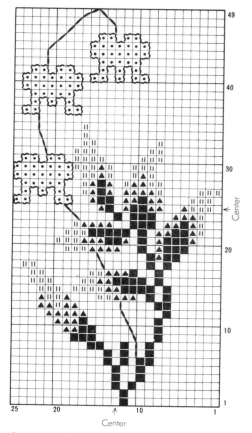

One square of design equals one square mesh of fabric.

Color Key   Use 4 strands of floss.
                  Required amount is shown in brackets.

Green

⬛ = 3345 ⎫
◥ = 3345 Holbein st. ⎬ [0.5 skein]
▲ = 992 [Small amount]
ⅠⅠ = 704 [Small amount]

White • = [0.5 skein]

Black ⌐⌐ =   Holbein st. [Small amount]

Scissors Case (g) *shown on page 28.*

Materials:
Fabric: Cream Indian cloth (52 mesh to 10cm), 13.5cm by 13cm. Cotton fabric for lining, 13.5cm by 13cm.
Thread: D.M.C. 6-strand embroidery floss, No. 25. See the arrow for colors and amount.
Finished Size: 6.5cm by 13.5cm.
Directions: Embroider on front as indicated. Make up for scissors case following diagrams.

Fishbone St.

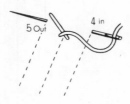

Actual Size

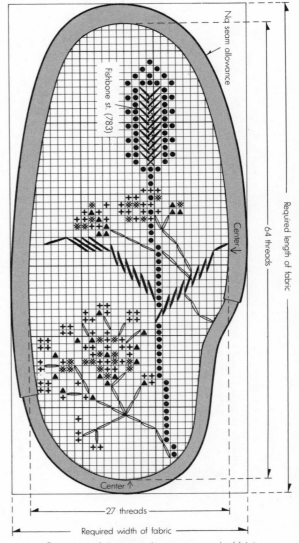

One square of design equals one square mesh of fabric.

※ Cut back piece, reversing pattern.
Cut fabric for lining same size as outer piece.

➡ **Color Key** Use 4 strands of floss.
Small amount each of following colors is required.

Shades of red
※ = 350
➕ = 351

Golden yellow
● = 783

◥ = 783
Straight st.

Scarab green
▲ = 3347

◩ = 3347
Holbein st.

98

How to make up:

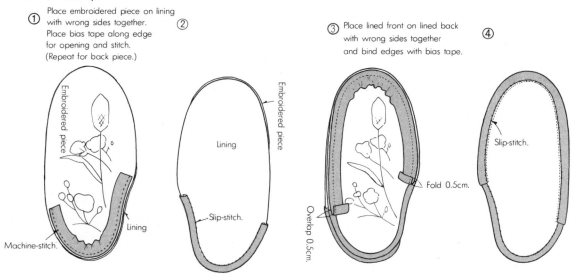

① Place embroidered piece on lining with wrong sides together. Place bias tape along edge for opening and stitch. (Repeat for back piece.)

②

③ Place lined front on lined back with wrong sides together and bind edges with bias tape.

④

Embroidered piece

Lining

Machine-stitch.

Lining

Embroidered piece

Lining

Slip-stitch.

Embroidered piece

Overlap 0.5cm.

Fold 0.5cm.

Slip-stitch.

Tissue Cases (c), (d) & (e) *shown on page 30.*

Materials (for one):
Fabric: Beige Indian cloth (52 mesh to 10cm), 20cm by 14cm. Organdy for lining, 20cm by 14cm.
Thread: D.M.C. 6-strand embroidery floss, No. 25. See the arrow for colors and amount.

Notions: Bias tape, 1.2cm wide and 28cm long.
Finished Size: 9cm by 12cm.
Directions: Match center of fabric and design, and embroider. Make up tissue case following diagrams.

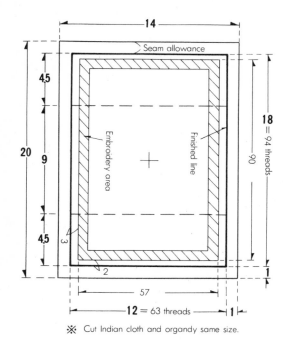

※ Cut Indian cloth and organdy same size.

How to make up:

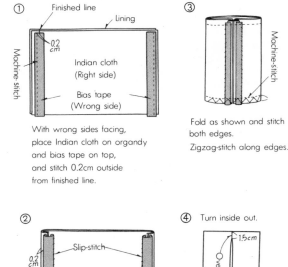

① Finished line

Lining

Machine stitch

0.2 cm

Indian cloth (Right side)

Bias tape (Wrong side)

With wrong sides facing, place Indian cloth on organdy and bias tape on top, and stitch 0.2cm outside from finished line.

③

Machine-stitch

Fold as shown and stitch both edges.
Zigzag-stitch along edges.

② 0.2 cm

Slip-stitch

Bias tape (Right side)

Turn bias tape to back and slip-stitch.

④ Turn inside out.

1.5cm

Overcast

1.5cm

Overcast 1.5cm each end.

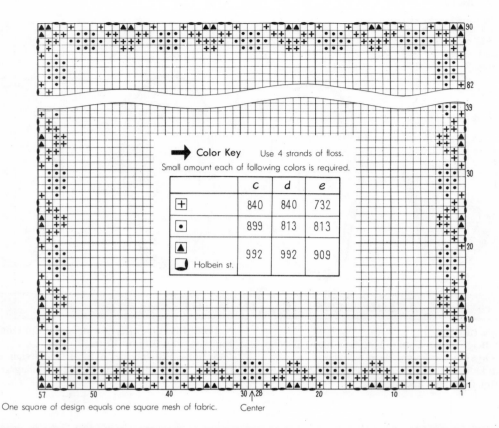

Color Key — Use 4 strands of floss.
Small amount each of following colors is required.

	c	d	e
+	840	840	732
•	899	813	813
▲	992	992	909
▢ Holbein st.			

One square of design equals one square mesh of fabric.

Center

Cosmetic Cases (f) & (g) *shown on pages 30 & 31.*

Materials (for one):
Fabric: Pink (blue) Indian cloth (52 mesh to 10cm), 44cm by 18.5cm. Cotton broadcloth for lining, 29cm by 19cm.
Thread: D.M.C. 6-strand embroidery floss, No. 25. See the arrow for colors and amount.

Notions: Zipper, 16cm long.
Finished Size: See diagram.
Directions: Match center of fabric and design, and cross-stitch. Make up cosmetic case following diagrams.

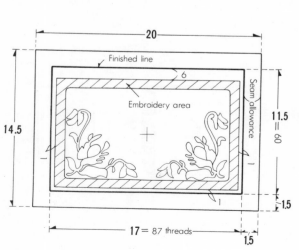

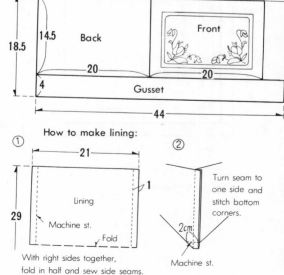

Cutting Layout

Back · Front · Gusset

How to make lining:

① With right sides together, fold in half and sew side seams.

② Turn seam to one side and stitch bottom corners.

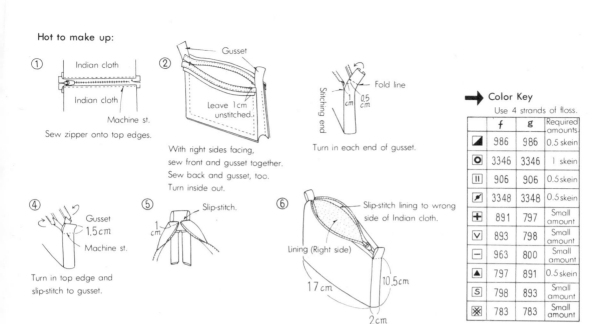

Hot to make up:

① Indian cloth / Indian cloth / Machine st.
Sew zipper onto top edges.

② Gusset / Leave 1cm unstitched.
With right sides facing, sew front and gusset together. Sew back and gusset, too. Turn inside out.

③ Stitching end / Fold line / 1cm / 0.5cm
Turn in each end of gusset.

④ Gusset 1.5cm / Machine st.
Turn in top edge and slip-stitch to gusset.

⑤ Slip-stitch. / 1cm

⑥ Slip-stitch lining to wrong side of Indian cloth. / Lining (Right side) / 17cm / 10.5cm / 2cm

Color Key
Use 4 strands of floss.

	f	g	Required amounts
◪	986	986	0.5 skein
◎	3346	3346	1 skein
‖	906	906	0.5 skein
◩	3348	3348	0.5 skein
✚	891	797	Small amount
V	893	798	Small amount
−	963	800	Small amount
▲	797	891	0.5 skein
S	798	893	Small amount
✕	783	783	Small amount

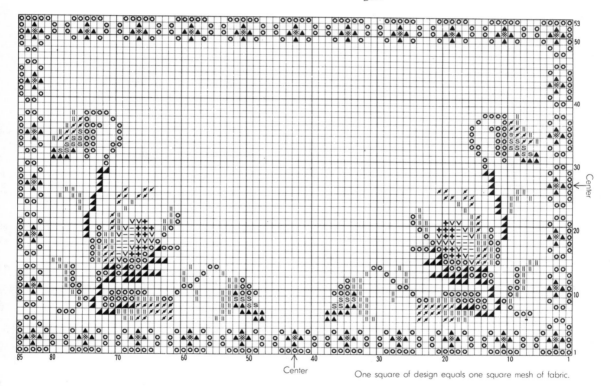

One square of design equals one square mesh of fabric.

Center

Cosmetic Cases (h), (i) & (j) shown on pages 30 & 31.

Materials (for one):
Fabric: Beige Indian cloth (52 mesh to 10cm), 33cm by 25.5cm for (h) and (i); 35cm by 18cm for (j). Cotton broadcloth for lining: 33cm by 25.5cm, for (h) and (i); 35cm by 18cm, for (j).
Thread: D.M.C. 6-strand embroidery floss, No. 25. See the arrow for colors and amount.
Notions: Zipper, 20cm long. Lace edging, 33cm long.
Finished Size: See diagram.
Directions: Match center of fabric and design, and cross-stitch. Make up crosmetic case following diagrams.

For (h) and (i)

Front and Back

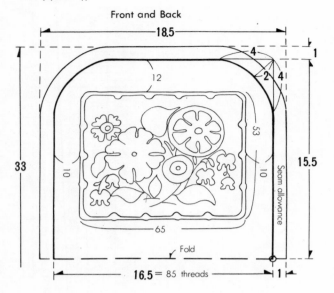

18.5

4
2 4
12

53

33

10

10

15.5

Seam allowance

1

65

Fold

16.5 = 85 threads

1

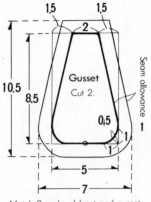

1.5   1.5

2

10.5   8.5

Gusset
Cut 2.

0,5

1

1

5

7

Match 0-marks of front and gusset.

※ Cut lining fabric (front and back, and gussets)
same size as outer pieces.

How to make up:

①
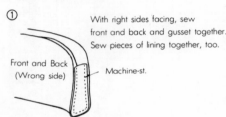

With right sides facing, sew
front and back and gusset together.
Sew pieces of lining together, too.

Front and Back
(Wrong side)

Machine-st.

②
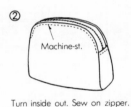

Machine-st.

Turn inside out. Sew on zipper.

③
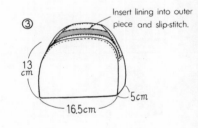

Insert lining into outer
piece and slip-stitch.

13 cm

5 cm

16.5 cm

For (j)

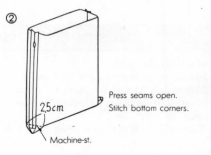

How to make up: With right sides facing, fold in half
crosswise and sew side seams.

18

1

1

1

Casing

5.5 cm

42

35

Seam allowance

16.5

14

14

Finished line

55

Fold

16 = 83 threads

1

①
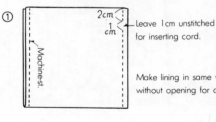

2 cm
1 cm

Leave 1cm unstitched
for inserting cord.

Machine-st.

Make lining in same way
without opening for cord.

②

2.5 cm

Press seams open.
Stitch bottom corners.

Machine-st.

※ Cut lining pieces same size as outer ones.

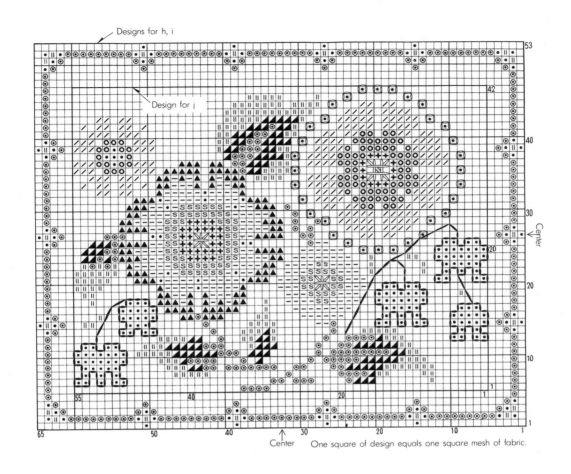

Designs for h, i

Design for j

53
42
40
30
20
20
10
1

Center

55 40 20 1

65 50 40 30 20 10 1

Center One square of design equals one square mesh of fabric.

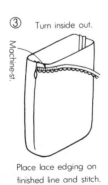

③ Turn inside out.

Machine-st.

Place lace edging on finished line and stitch.

④ Insert lining into outer piece and slip-stitch.

Casing

Machine-st.

Insert lining into outer piece, turn in seam allowance and slip-stitch along top edge. Machine-stitch for casing.

Cord:
Ch with 9 strands of 3m-long Jade green (943) embroidery floss.

Tie each end.

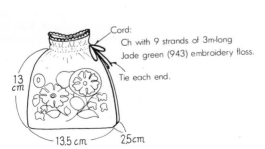

13 cm

13.5 cm 2.5 cm

Color Key   Use 4 strands of floss.

	h	i	j	Required amounts
◣	905	991	991	Small amount
◉	3345	943	943	h, i 0.5 skein j 1.5 skeins
‖ ◥ Holbein st.	703	703	703	0.5 skein
▲	553	971	798	Small amount
S	718	741	799	"
—	603	743	996	"
O	806	335	718	"
/	807	957	603	"
+	550	921	792	"
• ✳ Double cross st. ⬚ Four-sided st. (See page 36)	White	White	White	0.5 skein

Materials:
Fabric: Navy Indian cloth (52 mesh to 10cm), 90cm by
46cm. Cotton broadcloth for lining, 90cm by 48cm.
Thread: D.M.C. 6-strand embroidery floss, No. 25. See

the arrow for colors and amount.
Notions: Iron-on interfacing, 90cm by 35cm.
Finished Size: See diagram.

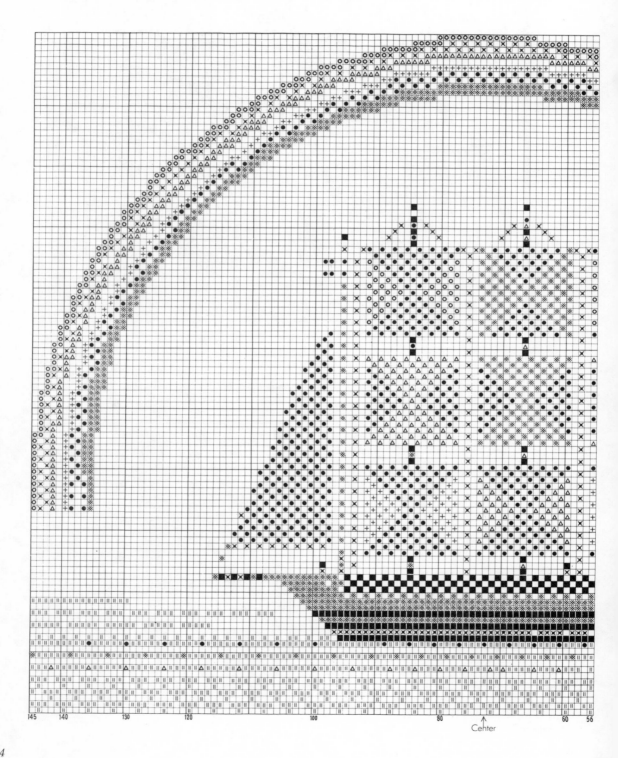

Directions: Match center of fabric and design, and cross-stitch. Press iron-on interfacing onto wrong side of embroidered piece. Sew front and back pieces together with right sides facing. Turn to right side. Turn in top edge and sew handles in place. Sew pocket onto back piece of lining. Sew front and back pieces of lining together. Insert lining into outer piece and slip-stitch.

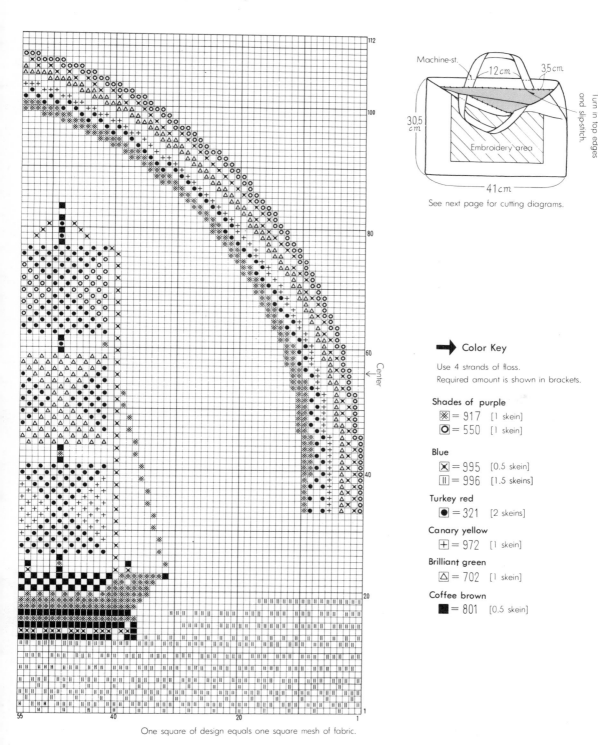

One square of design equals one square mesh of fabric.

Machine-st.
12 cm
3.5 cm
30.5 cm
Embroidery area
Turn in top edges and slip-stitch.
41 cm

See next page for cutting diagrams.

➡ Color Key

Use 4 strands of floss.
Required amount is shown in brackets.

Shades of purple
⊠ = 917 [1 skein]
Ⓞ = 550 [1 skein]

Blue
☒ = 995 [0.5 skein]
Ⅲ = 996 [1.5 skeins]

Turkey red
● = 321 [2 skeins]

Canary yellow
⊞ = 972 [1 skein]

Brilliant green
△ = 702 [1 skein]

Coffee brown
■ = 801 [0.5 skein]

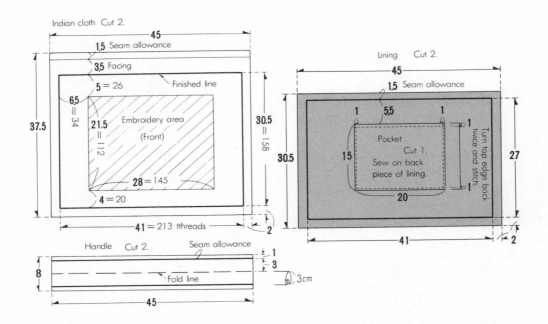

Indian cloth Cut 2.

45

1.5 Seam allowance

3.5 Facing

5 = 26

6.5 = 34

21.5 = 112

Embroidery area
(Front)

Finished line

37.5

30.5 = 158

30.5

28 = 145

4 = 20

41 = 213 threads

2

Lining   Cut 2.

45

1.5 Seam allowance

1   5.5   1

1

Pocket
Cut 1.
Sew on back
piece of lining.

15

20

1

27

Turn top edge back
twice and stitch.

30.5

41

2

Handle   Cut 2.

Seam allowance

8

Fold line

1
3

3cm

45

Shoulder Bag (a) *shown on page 32.*

Materials:
Fabric: Brown Java canvas (41 mesh to
10cm), 60cm by 25.5cm. Cotton broadcloth for lining, 65cm by 24cm.
Thread: D.M.C. 6-strand embroidery
floss, No. 25. See the arrow for colors and
amount
Notions: Iron-on interfacing, 48cm by
22cm. Cotton cord, 0.8cm in diameter and
140cm long. Small amount of Velcro.
Finished Size: See diagram.
Directions: Match center of front and
design, and cross-stitch. Press iron-on
interfacing on wrong side of embroidered
piece. Make up shoulder bag following
diagrams.

Indian cloth Cut 2.

25.5

1.5 Seam allowance

3 Facing

12

Embroidery area
(Front of Indian cloth)

76

30

23.5 = 96 threads

Seam allowance

76

8

21.5 = 88 threads

2

Lining   Cut 2.

25.5

Seam allowance 1.5cm

2

Pocket
Sew on back
piece of lining.

10

12

24

20.5

Seam allowance

21.5

2

Add 1.5cm for seam allowance to top edge
and 1cm each to three sides.

How to make up:

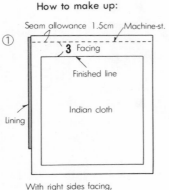

Seam allowance 1.5cm   Machine-st.

①

3 Facing

Finished line

Indian cloth

Lining

With right sides facing,
sew outer piece and lining together.
Turn seams to outer piece.
Sew pieces for back pieces together.

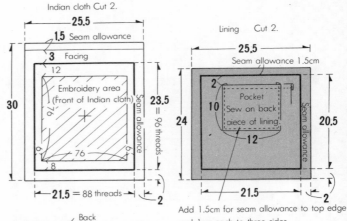

Back

②

13.5

Opening for turning

Pocket

Lining

Front

① Sew front and back together with right sides facing,
leaving opening for turning.

Indian cloth

Machine-st.

③

0.6 Machine-st.

Turn inside out.
Slip-stitch opening closed.
Machine-stitch along top edge.

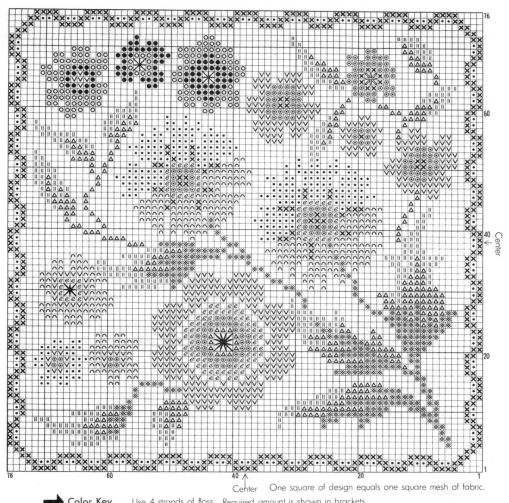

One square of design equals one square mesh of fabric.

Color Key   Use 4 strands of floss. Required amount is shown in brackets.

Shades of pink
● = 351 [0.5 skein]
○ = 353 [0.5 skein]

Shades of yellow
ℓ = 741 [0.5 skein]
V = 743 [1 skein]

Shades of green
✻ = 987 [1 skein]
△ = 3346 [1 skein]
‖ = 471 [1 skein]

Shades of brown
✕ = 435 [1 skein]
∩ = 739 [1 skein]

Corn yellow
· = 712 [1 skein]

Fire red
◉ = 947 [0.5 skein]

Double cross st.
✳ = 743   ✕ = 3346
✳ = 435

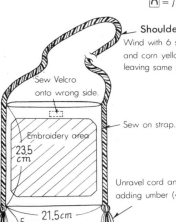

Shoulder strap:
Wind with 6 strands each of umber (435)
and corn yellow (712) alternately,
leaving same space for each,

Sew Velcro onto wrong side.

Sew on strap.

Embroidery area
23.5 cm

Unravel cord and make tassel,
adding umber (435) and corn yellow (712).

21.5cm

5 cm

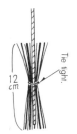

12 cm

Tie tight.

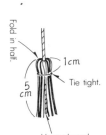

Fold in half.

1cm

Tie tight.

5 cm

Unravel cord and trim ends.

BASICS IN CROSS-STITCH

FABRICS

The exact amount of the fabric to make each project is given in this book. Make sure to buy enough fabric, allowing for shrinkage or difference of thread count.

Fineness or coarseness of the fabric will determine the finished size of the design.

To make the project the size shown in the book, use fabric with same gauge (the number of vertical and horizontal threads per 10cm square is given in the book). If you use coarser fabric than indicated, the finished size will be bigger and you may need more fabric. There are several kinds of fabric suitable for cross-stitch embroidery.

Cotton and linen fabrics on which you can count the threads easily are used most. Woolen and polyester fabrics are also used. Choose the most suitable even-weave fabric for your project.

Indian cloth and Java canvas are woven with several threads to each warp and weft. They are the most suitable fabrics for cross-stitch embroidery.

Congress canvas in woven with a single thick thread, thus this is a heavy-weight canvas. It is often used for cross-stitch embroidery and free-style embroidery with large stitches. Light-weight congress canvas is used for tablecloths with complicated embroidery.

Oxford cloth is often used for counted thread embroidery. This is an even-weave fabric and has double threads.

Even-weave linen comes in various thickness from fine to coarse. Light-weight linen is used for table linens with fine embroidery.

Length of Thread:

Use thread of 50cm length at a time, since longer thread may be tangled or twisted, which causes poor results and also causes the thread to lose its shine.

Starting Point:

Count the threads of the fabric and mark the starting point or center of design with colored thread. Make sure to count the threads of the fabric when embroidering repeating or symmetrical patterns.

THREADS

There are various kinds of threads used, depending on the thickness of the fabric.

Six-strand embroidery floss, No. 25, is most commonly used. Woolen yarn (tapestry yarn), and gold and silver threads are also used according to the texture of the fabric.

Six-strand embroidery floss, No. 25: This can be separated into one or more strands. When 3 strands of floss are required; for example, pull out one strand at a time and put three strands together. The length of one skein is 8 meters long.

Pearl cotton, No. 5: This is a shiny corded thread. The length of one skein is 25 meters long.

NEEDLES

You may use any needle for embroidery, but a blunt-pointed needle for cross-stitch embroidery is easiest to use. Change the size of the needle and the number of strands, depending on the fabric to be used.

To embroider with one strand of floss, use No. 23 needle for cross-stitch embroidery, and Nos. 19 and 20 needles for 4 to 6 strands of floss. Choose the proper needle and the number of strands suitable for the fabric and design.

Preparations:

The fabric suitable for cross-stitch embroidery frays easily, so overcast the edges with large stitches to prevent raveling.

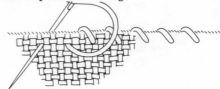

How to Thread:

Fold the thread over the end of the needle, slip it off with thumb and forefinger and push it through the needle eye.

Fold the thread end.

Slip it off with thumb and fore-finger.

To prevent the thread from twisting:

The thread is apt to twist while embroidering. To prevent this, turn the needle occasionally. Before starting, put the required number of strands together by pulling out one strand at a time from skein.

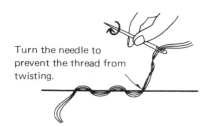

Turn the needle to prevent the thread from twisting.

Starting and Ending:

Leave the thread twice as long as the length of the needle on the wrong side when starting. After embroidering, weave the thread end into 2- to 3cm-stitches on the wrong side and clip off the excess thread. When you use various kinds of colored threads, weave and clip off any excess thread every time new thread is used.

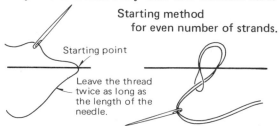

Starting method for even number of strands.

Starting point

Leave the thread twice as long as the length of the needle.

CROSS-STITCH

Make sure to work all the top threads of crosses in the same direction.
Never mix them up.

To work horizontally:

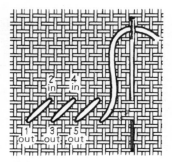

Bring the thread through on the lower left line of the cross. Insert the needle on the upper line a little to the right.

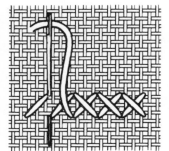

When coming to the end of the row, bring the thread through on the lower right line of the cross and insert the needle on the upper line a little to the left. Return in this way completing the other half of the cross.

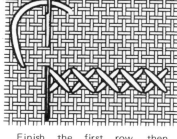

Finish the first row, then proceed to the next row.

To complete each cross horizontally:

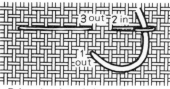

Bring the thread through on the lower left line of the cross. Take a small stitch from 2 to 3.

Insert the needle on the lower line a little to the right (at 4) emerging at 5.

Continue working horizontally completing each cross.

To complete each cross vertically:

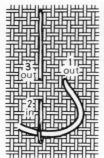

Bring the thread through on the upper right line of the cross. Take a stitch from 2 to 3.

Insert the needle on the lower line a little to the right emerging at 5.

Take a stitch from 6 to 7.

Continue working vertically, completing each cross. When you work downward, the stitches should cross in the same direction.

To work upward diagonally:

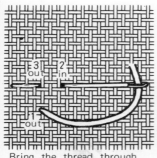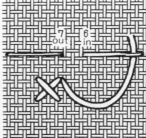

Bring the thread through at 1 and take a horizontal stitch from 2 to 3.

Take a vertical stitch from 4 to 5.

Continue working diagonally, completing each cross.

To work downward diagonally:

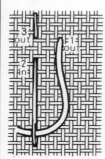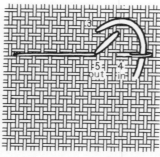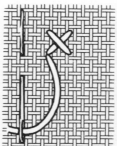

Bring the thread through at 1 and take a vertical stitch from 2 to 3.

Take a horizontal stitch from 4 to 5.

Continue working downward diagonally, completing each cross.

DOUBLE CROSS-STITCH

Work Cross-Stitch first. Then work another Cross-Stitch over the previous stitch as shown. All stitches should cross in the same way.

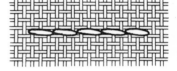

HOLBEIN STITCH

This is also called Line Stitch and is sometimes used as an outline to Cross-Stitch. The stitch is completed by working from left to right and coming back from right to left. Stitches on the wrong side are the same on the front.

Straight Line:

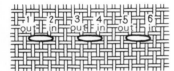

Work running stitch of equal length.

When you come to the end of the row, return in the same way filling in the spaces left by the first row. For a neater finish, work in the same way when you insert the needle and bring it through.

Diagonal Line:

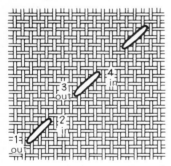

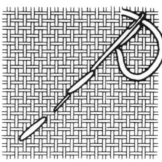

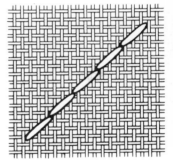

Work running stitch of equal length diagonally.

When you come to the end of the row, return in the same way filling in the spaces left by the first row.

Zigzag Line:

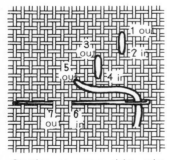

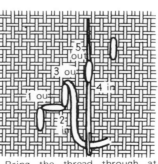

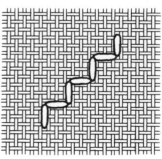

Starting at upper right, take vertical stitches diagonally.

Bring the thread through at 1 and take a horizontal stitch from 2 to 3.

Fill in the spaces with horizontal stitches to form zigzag line.